"I have been a minister for more than seventy-three years. In all of those years, I have been asked one question more than any other: 'Was Elvis ready to meet the Lord?' My answer: 'Only God, in his infinite wisdom, knows the heart and soul of each of us.' However, it was my privilege, along with my wife, Maude Aimee, to visit with Elvis on several occasions. On each of these occasions, we shared the living Word of God with Elvis Presley.

"His heart was open and warm to the seeds of the gospel that we tried to sow. He was full of questions concerning our Lord's soon return and how we would spend eternity with him at the right hand of the Father.

In this book, Joe Moscheo speaks of one of these occasions where we had the privilege to share the gospel with Elvis Presley. We were thrilled to know that Elvis held our ministry in such high esteem.

"As described in the pages of this book, my wife told Elvis she considered him her 'bell sheep.' When he asked what that meant, she had the opportunity to tell him about the shepherds in the Holy Land who tied a bell around the neck of one of their sheep. The rest of the flock would follow wherever they were led by the sound of the bell. Maude Aimee told Elvis that she was praying that Elvis would have a 'bell sheep' spiritual experience that would cause him to lead thousands of people to the Lord.

"No one knows the true heart of a man. However, as a minister of the gospel who has counseled and prayed with countless thousands of people in my years of ministry, I believe that someday we will meet Elvis just inside the eastern gates.

"My prayer is that God will bless this book and those who read it, drawing them ever closer to our wonderful Lord."

—*Rev. Rex Humbard*

"God blessed many kings on Earth, but perhaps none more than the King of Rock and Roll. That was probably because he loved the King of kings. I found this book to be a powerful, untold side of an icon who touched the lives of countless people.

"Who better to share this story with us than Joe, who shared Elvis' stage and his love of gospel music? This book is a fun, fascinating read I couldn't put down."

—*Stephen Baldwin, actor and author of The Unusual Suspect*

"Joe Moscheo has accomplished more things for gospel music than just about anyone I can think of. From his performance days with The Imperials to his work with Elvis and behind the scenes with The Gospel Music Association and The Gospel Music Hall of Fame, Joe has been a constant ambassador for gospel music. He is loved and respected in our community and has been an encouraging friend to countless artists and musicians. Joe Moscheo is a treasure in our business."

—*Michael W. Smith, singer, songwriter, producer*

"In 1971, I received a call from RCA records in Nashville telling me that not only did Elvis record my song 'He Touched Me,' but they were naming the album by that title. Needless to say I was both pleased and honored. My friend Joe Moscheo was there for those sessions, and now, in this book, he has focused on the importance of gospel music in Elvis' life. Everyone will find this a fascinating side that's been little known for too long."

—*Bill Gaither, gospel songwriter, singer, and producer*

THE GOSPEL SIDE OF

ELVIS

Joe Moscheo

with a Foreword by Priscilla Presley

CENTER
STREET®

NEW YORK BOSTON NASHVILLE

Unless otherwise listed, all Scripture references are taken from the
Holy Bible, New International Version (NIV), © 1973, 1978, and 1984,
The International Bible Society.
Used by permission of Zondervan Publishing House. All rights reserved.

All pull-quotes from *He Touched Me: The Gospel Music of Elvis Presley* DVD,
executive produced by Joe Moscheo.

Center Street
Hachette Book Group USA
237 Park Avenue
New York, NY 10017

Visit our Web site at www.centerstreet.com.

Center Street is a division of Hachette Book Group USA, Inc. The Center
Street name and logo is a trademark of Hachette Book Group USA, Inc.

Printed in the United States of America

First Edition: August 2007
10 9 8 7 6 5 4 3 2 1

Library of Congress Cataloging-in-Publication Data
Moscheo, Joe.
    The Gospel side of Elvis / Joe Moscheo. — 1st. ed.
        p. cm.
    Includes index.
    ISBN-13: 978-1-59995-729-6
    ISBN-10: 1-59995-729-9
    1. Presley, Elvis, 1935–1977. 2. Rock musicians—United States—Biography.
I. Title.

    ML420.P96M74 2007
    782.42166092—dc22
    [B]   2007006069

*I dedicate this book to my loving wife, Judy,
and to my children: Toni, Joe III, Gina, Mandi, Angela; to my
sister Mary Lou; to Darren and Gabriel; and to my grandchildren:
Mack, Adrienne, Emmie, Carlee, Frankie, and Jacob. Thank you for
your prayers, love, and support. I love each of you very much.*

Contents

FOREWORD

I have always felt this side of Elvis has never fully been explored—for it was truly the foundation of his style, his spirit, and his passion. Anyone who spent any time with Elvis realized very quickly how much gospel music was a part of him. Joe Moscheo's in-depth knowledge of Elvis' love of gospel gives the reader a wonderful history of his favorite singers, quartets, and groups. Joe shares with you stories that have not yet been so fully disclosed. Many of these stories are so vivid in my mind and are told with such eloquence and sentiment. Joe's thoughts and opinions of what he perceived or witnessed during his time with Elvis are well thought out and honest without harsh criticism, shared with compassion. His respect of Elvis is undoubtedly genuine.

Now, when one lived in Elvis' world, you shared his passions. Anything that Elvis loved, he wanted to share (well, almost anything). When he would sit at a piano, he would invariably choose a gospel song over a song a listener may think he would choose. We would attend the National Gospel Convention and inevitably make our way backstage where Elvis introduced me to all those he was influenced by and those he admired.

I lived and breathed gospel with him nearly every Sunday, beginning at six o'clock in the morning for years, listening to the Happy Goodman Family, the Blackwood Brothers, the Statesmen Quartet, the Stamps, and more. Elvis made sure he had my undivided attention as he would go through every performance and point out each band's qualities and what made each of them distinctive and great. He would have me listen to the highs and lows of a note that Jake Hess or J. D. Sumner would hit. And when he watched them sing, it was as if Elvis himself was on that stage singing with them. Elvis felt every single word and emotion being sung. Joe's recollections come firsthand. He experienced it by being around and traveling with Elvis. He lived it as one of The Imperials gospel quartet onstage with him, and now he shares it generously with you.

Enjoy.
Priscilla Presley

Preface

At last count, over one thousand books had been written about Elvis Presley. Why, you may ask, would I even attempt to write another? Well, even though I haven't read all of them (there are too many), I do know none of them have given enough attention and credence to the part of his life I like to call "the Gospel Side." Let me state at the very beginning of this book that I truly believe Elvis was the greatest gospel singer of all time. In these pages I will try to substantiate this belief. I hope to present a balanced account of his life and work, but from a different perspective: one that seeks to encourage his fans and others, and one stressing the positive aspects of his life. After all, that was the way I experienced Elvis. I want you to hear his story once again, but this time as if you were standing beside me.

I wasn't privileged to be around him on a daily basis; I didn't live with him at Graceland, or even close by. I was never on call twenty-four hours a day, like most of the guys in his immediate group, sometimes known as "the Memphis Mafia." I wasn't on a weekly salary, and didn't get to hang out with him most days and nights, or witness his mood swings. I never saw firsthand some of the images of Elvis portrayed to us by those who were there on a more constant basis: impatient, imposing, sometimes irrational, demanding, earnestly searching, confused—and the list goes on. I was there for a limited amount of time, and for weeks, rather than months or years at a time, but I liked what I saw. Elvis had a way about him; he could win you in a second and hang on to you for years. I observed a lot from a unique perspective, and it seems to me there are only a few of us left who share my commitment to this part of his story, only a handful of us who experienced life with Elvis from this point of view.

Elvis was a once-in-a-lifetime happening. You could say he was a special, or a chosen, or a called individual. I don't expect to see his like again in my life. Now, thirty years after his passing, I finally feel comfortable enough to say the things found in this book, and to make the statements describing my beliefs about Elvis Presley. I knew these things then, when I was performing with him, but the impressions have become even stronger as the years go by. His music endures and is more meaningful than ever; his gospel music lives on; the message has never ceased being relevant and continues to touch the lives and hearts of all who hear it.

As I recall these events and stories—some witnessed firsthand, and some told over and over again—I hope to give you a sense of why this interpretation of him was so important to me, and will be for a lot of others. After keeping pretty quiet for all these years, now the timing seems right for me to share the impact Elvis and his music had on my life, an impact and influence that has become as much a part of me as my own skin. I offer these presumptions, opinions, and feelings as nothing other than my own, and from my heart.

ACKNOWLEDGMENTS

I t will be impossible for me to thank everyone for the parts they've played in making this book possible, all the musicians and singers through the years, and all the caring and sensitive individuals who knew this was an important "side" to talk about, that this message needed to be heard. I am deeply grateful for all the thoughts and prayers. Even though your names may not appear here, your support and passion have been felt throughout this process.

I've enjoyed a close relationship with Priscilla, and consider her a great friend and a beautiful lady—someone I admire very much. Thank you for our friendship all these years. I really haven't been around Lisa Marie in a long time, but I've watched her grow, and see so much of her dad in her; she is so talented and giving. I've also enjoyed a long friendship with Colonel and Mrs. Beaulieu and Michele Hovey. Jack Soden and my good buddy Gary Hovey have been so gracious to me and have always extended the sort of kind consideration that made me feel like an "insider." Todd Morgan, thanks for listening, for your help, and for your interest in this subject.

I'd also like to acknowledge and say a special thank-you to the "Original Cast" from the Vegas years: James Burton, Ronnie Tutt, Glen D. Hardin, Jerry Scheff, John Wilkinson, Joe Guercio, Myrna Smith, Estelle Brown, Sylvia Shemwell, Cissy Houston, Millie Kirkham, Armond Morales, Jim Murray, Terry Blackwood, Roger Wiles, Greg Gordon, Sherman Andrus, Ed Enoch, Ed Hill, Donnie Sumner, Bill Baize, Larry Strickland, Richard Sterban, Sherrill Nielson, Tim Beatty, and Tony Brown. A grateful nod of appreciation for paving the way for all of us goes to the Jordanaires, especially Gordon Stoker and Ray Walker.

To all the Gospel Greats who have gone on: Jake Hess, J. D. Sumner, Hovie Lister, James Blackwood, Charlie Hodge, the Matthews brothers, Neal Mathews, Hoyt Hawkins, "Big Chief" Wetherington—E.P. loved and was inspired by all of these guys.

Thank you to the group of family members and close friends who were there on a daily basis to watch over him, the Memphis Mafia: Joe, Red, Sonny, Lamar, Jerry, George, Alan, Richard, Billy, Dick, Sam, Dave, Charlie, Mike, Jimmy, Marty, Gene, David, Rick, and Ray.

To Terry Blackwood, Sherman Andrus, and Gus Gaches, thank you for making me sound good and for these added years we've had together; your lives are a blessing to me.

A huge thanks goes to Stig Edgren for making it possible for us to see it all again with *Elvis, the Concert*. Thanks to my good friend and partner in crime, Joe Guercio: it's been great fun, even after all these years!

I offer my thanks to all the faithful fans and fan clubs around the world: your loyalty and support are the heartbeat that keeps us all going, especially the clubs in America, Belgium, England,

Germany, Italy, Holland, Denmark, France—uh-oh, this wasn't such a good idea; I might forget someone! I thank you all for keeping this legend alive.

To my comrades at Gaither Productions, Barry Jennings and Bill Carter: thank you for including me.

To Didier Thielens, my Web-master: thank you for all your hard work.

To the stellar group of people at Hachette Book Group USA and Center Street, especially to Cara Highsmith for introducing this idea and for being a part of my family for almost twenty years; to my senior editor, Gary Terashita: without your fervent belief and wisdom, I would have given up. I've learned so much from you; thank you for grounding me, and keeping me focused. I'm also grateful to the terrific team who will market and sell this book to the fans, and new friends, around the world.

Finally to Thom Lemmons, whose words made this come alive, and who "got it" immediately. Your experience as a writer, your knowledge of music, your energy, and your enthusiasm for the subject made me dig a little deeper each time. I couldn't have done it without you; I appreciate you very much.

THE GOSPEL SIDE OF

ELVIS

Introduction

SHOW PROCEDURE TOUR

(No Elvis music in P.A. prior to show)

Elvis Presley Picture Sou. Albums on sale Thru out audience

Off Stage - 1st Announcement will be pitches for pictures and

books. Each 15 minutes starting 1 hour before show time.

at 8:25 or 5 minutes prior to show time announcements made

regarding security requirements. No one can leave seats

or move beyond first row or stand in aisles or it will be

necessary to stop the show. Also, a fine group of acts

are here to present the best possible show so please give

them your courteous attention... ~~In a moment~~ *In a moment a Two our show will begin*

to start the show

And now, here is our musical conductor, Joe Guercio, to get

the show off to a swinging beginning

After applause *Drump Roll*——————

Off Stage: We now present the IMPERIALS ....

Enter to Music. Go into first number.

(after first number Hugh introduces self as M.C. for

show and then introduces second number.)

Exit to applause. House spots on the act exiting to enable

Inspiration musicians to be moving into position. (Their

amps turned on before the show) Also four microphones put

in position for Sweet Inspirations.

SHOW PROCEDURE TOUR   Pg. 2

Off Stage Announcement: And now, Ladies and Gentlemen,

    The Sweet Inspirations.

After last number - Sweet Inspirations will exit to music.

    House lights again down to exit Sweet Inspirations and

    musicians.

Spots directed to stage to pick up Sammy Shore.

    Off Stage Announcement: And now we're proud to present,

    The Comedy star Jouy   - Mr. Sammy Shore.

Sammy does act and house band plays off. The final chord of

    first half of show.

                    HOUSE LIGHTS UP - INTERMISSION

Off Stage: Advise 15 minute intermission

    Refreshments available.

    Plug pictures and books.

Elvis show To PORTLAND, SEATTLE
AND BACK TO SAN FRANCISCO
Cow PALACE on Friday Nov. 13th
Lots of Good seats For
THAT SHOW Are AVAILABLE.

Poster → 2.00
Portraits /
1414 Pictures → 1.00
+ Photo album /

ELVIS HAS Left The BuiLDING

Comfortable for everyone
observe the no smoking
rule in this seating area.
Smoking is permitting on
the outer concourses

SHOW PROCEDURE TOUR   Page 3

Off Stage: Two minutes prior to start of second half of
     show Hugh again advises no one getting in aisles,
     leaving their seats or approaching the stage. We want
     to make it possible for everyone to enjoy the show.

No More - Then house lights down - Elvis' musicians will move
     into positions. Their instruments set and turned on
     during intermission.

Stage stays completely dark as Joe Guercio and Elvis' band
     go into rhythm pattern. Lamar will then direct all
     spots to Elvis' entry position.

Lighting once Elvis enters will be as Lamar calls it.

Elvis if closing with CAN'T HELP FALLING IN LOVE can keep
     Elvis only spotted on last portion of song he sings -
     then fade into dark so he can exit rapidly and the
     band and singers continue with the closing tag of
     the song.

     Joe Guercio - band tag.

Ladies and Gentlemen - Elvis has left the building.

1969 -

A lmost everybody has an "Elvis" story. Let me tell you mine.

Pick any of several nights in the late 1960s and early 1970s. Place yourself inside any of the huge auditoriums scattered across this country, those places capable of holding 5,000, 10,000, 20,000 screaming fans. The concert is over; the adrenaline rush of watching the fast-paced, dazzling performance is beginning to ebb. And then, the booming voice of the announcer fills the vast spaces inside the concert hall: "Ladies and gentlemen, Elvis has left the building." It's a signal to the last lingerers and hangers-on that they might as well go on home, or to whatever other after-hours pursuits they've planned for this very special evening. Their idol, the one they came to see, to be mesmerized and transported by, isn't here anymore. Elvis has left the building.

Now imagine a different scene, a couple of hours earlier: You are sitting in a dressing room or a greenroom, the pre-performance nervous energy surging through your veins. You are about to go onstage in front of thousands of people, singing

7

backup for one of the world's most recognizable and popular entertainers. At certain moments, you can't believe you're actually here, and you certainly can't comprehend the sequence of events landing you in this place, but you are oh, so glad to be experiencing this moment.

Someone walks up to you, taps you on the shoulder. "You coming up to the suite, later?" he asks. "Elvis wants to know."

"Oh, yeah, sure. Is everybody coming?" You ask this question more from habit than anything else; you know that if the situation is typical, there will be perhaps dozens of musicians and friends gathered in Elvis' suite within an hour of the final curtain.

"Yeah, I think the Sweets are coming, and some of the guys in the TCB Band. Jim, Terry . . . you know. Why don't you come?"

"Absolutely. Tell Elvis I'll be there."

The guy nods. "Okay, great. Do good out there, okay?"

"Yeah, thanks."

He walks away. When he has gone, you allow yourself a tiny grimace, knowing you have just been invited—well, more like summoned, really—to attend a session that could last until the wee hours of the morning, or even past sunup. You know you must call your wife, who is waiting back in a hotel room with three small children, and explain to her, as you have done so many times before, "I'm sorry, honey, but Elvis feels like singing tonight. Don't wait up for me; I've got to go."

On many occasions, I was the backup singer in the scene you just read. I had the good fortune—I would even go so far as to call it the blessing—of touring and performing with Elvis as a member of The Imperials gospel quartet. We sang backup for Elvis in many of his most memorable performances and recordings. Because of this, I witnessed firsthand a side of Elvis Presley that may surprise you. The Elvis to whom I am referring was not the King of Rock and Roll, clad in a dazzling white jumpsuit and glittering with metal studs and stones of every color—though that charismatic performer was a part of the man I knew. It's not even the smiling, charming on-screen Elvis of *The Trouble with Girls* and *G.I. Blues*, though the native good looks and unassuming grin that made him so bankable at the box office reflected a genuine side of his character as well.

I want to introduce you to Elvis Presley, the lifelong devotee of gospel music. This was the music that lay closest to the heart and soul of this poor boy from Tupelo, Mississippi. Gospel music, both white Southern gospel and African American gospel, was the first music Elvis knew, and it was etched as indelibly on him as his fingerprints or the shape of his face. When he left the building, most nights, Elvis wanted nothing more than to go somewhere with a few friends and a piano, a place they could gather to sing and listen to the gospel music that nourished the heart and soul of this American musical and cultural icon.

That's the Elvis Presley I was privileged to know: the generous, humble man who could never quite get his mind around the fame and glitter which came his way; the friend who would do anything within his power to help you with a problem; the devoted son who never forgot the spiritual heritage instilled in him by a loving mother. That's the side of Elvis I'd like to introduce to you: the gospel side of Elvis.

. . . .

A FEW YEARS AGO, I helped produce a two-part documentary, *He Touched Me: The Gospel Music of Elvis Presley*. Due to the tremendous reception of that program, and in recognition of the thirtieth anniversary of Elvis' death in 2007, I began to think about ways to bring to a wider public this little-known side of a man I admire so much. There are so many stories, so many images, so many memories that could find a place in a story like this. Also, there are so many things already said and shown about Elvis. With everything written about Elvis Aaron Presley, some might wonder what could be left to say.

I offer two verses as a point of departure for this journey of discovery to which I'm inviting you. The first is from the Bible, possibly taught to Elvis by his mother, Gladys, who always made time for Bible instruction, both at home and in their church. The verse is this: "Train a child in the way he should go, and when he is old he will not turn from it" (Proverbs 22:6, NIV). Gladys Presley raised her son to be a churchgoing, Christian young man. Now, if all you think about is the glitz and showbiz and some of the craziness you've read about that came to symbolize Elvis' public career, this notion may seem far-fetched. But consider: The record on the turntable in his bedroom, possibly the last music Elvis Presley listened to before his untimely death, was an acetate recording of three of his favorite gospel songs, specially compiled by his lifelong friend and mentor, J. D. Sumner. Elvis never forgot his spiritual heritage. Somewhere, beyond all the dazzling lights and the flashy capes and the limousines and the throngs of screaming fans, his mind and heart returned again and again to the simple tenets taught to him at an early age by his mother. Gladys Presley trained him up, and I believe, in his heart of hearts, he never turned.

The second verse that points the way on our exploration of Elvis' life is a lyric from one of his famous gospel recordings written by Doris Akers: "Lead me, guide me along the way / For if you lead me, I cannot stray." There was, and remains strong in my mind to this day, the overwhelming belief that Elvis was intensely aware of divine influence and guidance for his life. So many times, at critical and even mundane points in his life, he would wonder out loud, "Why has all this come my way?" The fame, the fans, the wealth—Elvis often found it rather confusing. And in his confusion, he turned in the direction his heritage dictated: he turned to God. When Elvis sang the words "He touched me / and made me whole," more was happening than the manipulation of a lyric and a melody by a talented performer. When Elvis performed the hymn "How Great Thou Art" in his famous Las Vegas show or on one of his concert tours, the power of his delivery was due to much more than the calculation and training of a seasoned performer. As I and so many others who were close to him can attest, Elvis really believed the truth of words like these.

Consider these facts: Of all the records by Elvis Presley, the only three Grammy Awards he ever won were for gospel music. He recorded more gospel and inspirational songs than any pop performer before or since. Could these details possibly be due to mere coincidence, or is there a deeper reason, one that tells us something about the deepest motivations and interests of the man beneath the legend?

I hope you enjoy this fresh look at Elvis Presley. I offer it with the sincere wish that the public could know just a bit of the man I came to know: a warm, sincere man who did his best, admittedly imperfectly, not to permit his overwhelming fame to come between himself and those he cared about. Elvis was one of the most unremittingly public figures who has ever existed. In many ways, the image he projected—and the image projected onto him by the millions who adored him—has overtaken the human side of this shy boy who was ashamed of the shabby clothing he had to wear to school, but who rose to become one of the most influential figures in the history of popular music and culture, not to mention one of the most fabulously wealthy performers in the world. Because of the sheer size of his legacy and legend, it is almost inevitable that some have chosen to focus on their perceptions of his weaknesses and flaws. Having spent the amount of time I did near the whirl of activity and glamour surrounding Elvis, I am all too aware of his human frailties—as I am of my own.

But that isn't the story I want to tell. Instead, I want to focus on one particular facet of his life, one I believe has not received enough attention when compared with other aspects. I believe this story is an important key to understanding one of the things that made Elvis great. I believe that, more than any other single influence, the spiritual and religious heritage embodied in the words and rhythms of Southern and African American gospel music captured Elvis' imagination and guided his musical conception. Gospel music was the first music Elvis ever heard, and he was never free from its influences. It was imprinted on him almost from birth, and throughout his life, it was the place he returned to again and again for musical, emotional, and spiritual refreshment. These were the songs that carried him through hard times. And in a very real way, as you'll see, these were the songs that carried him home.

I attend and perform at dozens of Elvis-related events each

year, both in this country and internationally. At each show, we offer a question-and-answer session, and what I'm most frequently asked, especially by the Christian folks in the audience, is my opinion of whether Elvis was a true believer. "Do you think Elvis was a Christian?" they want to know. "Do you think Elvis is in heaven?" Before I go any further with this book, I want to try to lay my cards on the table with readers: I am not Elvis' judge. That job belongs to God alone. I have opinions about what I saw when I was a close associate and fellow performer, and I certainly have no wish to make any negative statements about him—or about anyone else, for that matter. As I stated earlier, much has been said and written about Elvis' faults and mistakes. And, to be honest, I'm too busy trying to tend to my own spiritual life to spend a lot of time pointing out the flaws in someone else's— especially someone I admired and considered to be a friend.

One way I've tried to explain all this to myself is in some words I heard attributed to a minister at a funeral for a church member whose life proved too much for him. Standing over the coffin of a man who had tried—and failed—to kick the habit that eventually killed him, this preacher said, "I didn't lose the same battles he did. But then, I wasn't in the same war."

As I think about Elvis' life, that statement makes a lot of sense to me. Yes, Elvis made some good decisions, and he made a number of bad ones. He brought joy to the lives of millions of people, and for some he fell short. Toward the end of his life, many of us who cared about him were very concerned, believing we saw a great weight of sadness, depression, and despair pressing him down more and more. He lost some battles I didn't have to fight. But he was in a different war. Did he fight the good fight? That's for God to say.

Another question worth asking is this: How do we measure the impact of a human life? Elvis' impact on the world of music is almost immeasurable; it is still evident today. Do we assess Elvis by the way his life ended, or by his entire life? Only God can look at the totality of a human heart, but I can personally attest to the good things I saw Elvis do, the generous acts I witnessed, and the intentions and beliefs I heard him express. Does that mean I know any more about Elvis' eternal destiny than anyone else? No. But as you hear his story through my words, it's possible you may come to see, as I did, that there was more than one side to this man who was adored by millions but known by only a few.

Let me introduce you to the Elvis Presley I was privileged to know. Let me try to reveal to you the gospel side of Elvis.

Chapter One

A Shared Passion

Had I sat down in the late 1950s to make a list of the events least likely to take place in my life, somewhere at the top I would have written the words, *Meeting Elvis Presley*. Think about it: How would a nice Italian boy from upstate New York ever expect even to so much as shake hands with the new sensation from Memphis, the guy whose voice was being heard on radios and record players all across America? And yet, not only did I eventually meet him, I was one of the fifty or so people on the planet who actually had the opportunity to share his stage—to perform with arguably the greatest entertainer of all time.

The answer, I've concluded, lies at least partly in the interest that brought us together: our shared passion for gospel music. But that answer opens up a few other questions. First, how did that nice Italian boy from upstate New York ever come in contact with Southern gospel music in the first place? What was the road that led from Albany and a budding career as a jazz pianist to Ellis Auditorium and the National Quartet Convention in

Memphis? And once I got there, why should I have expected to meet Elvis Presley—not only meet him, in fact, but realize he already knew who I was and what I was doing? Let me take you on a little journey and try to give you a glimpse of how this strange, unexpected path began to unfold.

THE ULTIMATE BEGINNING of the story lies in the origins of Southern gospel and quartet-style singing. In the late nineteenth and early twentieth centuries, singing schools, based on the "shape-note" system of musical notation, became a huge feature of the Southern religious scene. The hardworking, plain, mostly rural people who made up the majority of conservative Southern churches wanted to learn how to sing in worship, yet didn't have the time or the money to take formal musical training. Shape notes evolved as a system that could be easily learned in a weekend, or sometimes a weeklong singing school, organized and led by traveling teachers. They were called "shape notes" because the different notes of the scale each had a different shape. The musical style emphasized four-part harmony and the message of the songs was usually focused on some aspect of the Christian life or the hope of heaven.

The shape of each note, not their position on the staff, determined the sound of the note. The note sounded the same regardless of the key, following this scale:

Do Re Mi Fa Sol La Ti Do   Do Re Mi Fa Sol La Ti Do

Image source: http://www.paperlesshymnal.com/shapnote/shaped.htm

Here is an example of how this system is used in a hymnal:

36
CM
John Newton, 1779
St. 6, *Collection of Sacred Ballads*, 1790

Amazing Grace!

NEW BRITAIN
Shaw's & Spilman's *Columbian Harmony*, 1829
Arr., Edwin O. Excell, 1910

1. A - maz - ing grace! How sweet the sound– That saved a wretch like me!
2. 'Twas grace that taught my heart to fear, And grace my fears re - lieved;
3. Thro' man - y dan - gers, toils and snares, I have al - read - y come;
4. The Lord has prom - ised good to me: His Word my hope se - cures;
5. And when this flesh and heart shall fail, And mor - tal life shall cease,
6. When we've been there ten thou - sand years, Bright shin - ing as the sun,

I once was lost, but now am found– Was blind, but now I see.
How pre - cious did that grace ap - pear The hour I first be - lieved!
'Tis grace has brought me safe thus far, And grace will lead me home.
He will my shield and por - tion be As long as life en - dures.
I shall pos - sess with - in the veil A life of joy and peace.
We've no less days to sing God's praise Than when we've first be - gun.

"Convention songs" were the most difficult and complex music in the style, alternating between verse sections with all four parts singing the same basic rhythm and a chorus featuring independent, rhythmically challenging lines for each voice. They came to be called convention songs because they were often learned at the large gatherings organized to bring singers together from a wide area for the purpose of improving their skills and learning new songs. Much of the favorite repertoire of the male quartets was drawn from the convention song style, since the snappy rhythms and cross-accents tended to be crowd-pleasers. The early quartets, not surprisingly, were often sponsored by music publishing companies such as the Stamps-Baxter, Vaughn, or Rodeheaver organizations; the popularity of the quartets led directly to increased participation in singing schools and brisker sales of sheet music and hymnals. In the 1920s and 1930s, radio proved the perfect medium for bringing the music of the quartets to a larger public.

My father came to the United States from Sicily with his parents because their Pentecostal faith made them an object of persecution by the Roman Catholic majority. When I was a boy, he was pastoring a small, bilingual church in Albany, New York. Our family was always musical: My father played the violin and sang the songs he learned as a boy in Sicily, and by the time I was in high school I knew music would be my life's work.

My parents recognized and valued my interest in music. My father, of course, hoped I would learn enough piano to be able to play in church. They made great financial sacrifices. My mother, for example, took in washing and ironing in order to allow me to take lessons at a local conservatory. This experience confirmed to me that music was my ticket out of town. I progressed rapidly, and before long I was playing piano with a local jazz trio—not exactly the setting my father would have preferred. In fact, I never actually played piano for Dad's church.

After graduating from high school, I attended a small religious college in the South—a long way from Albany, New York, both in geography and culture. But there I met the girl I would later marry, and there I first heard the music that would transform my life and provide my introduction to the man who became the pivotal force in popular music history, Elvis Presley.

One night there was an event in a nearby town billed as an "All-Night Singing." This was a common feature of the gospel circuit: a promoter would book a hall and invite quartets to attend, then sell tickets to the event. The quartets would be paid from the gate proceeds, and, naturally, the more famous quartets with the large followings would command larger appearance fees than the lesser-known groups. Additionally, groups who had records and sheet music would sell them to eager gospel music fans.

To my delight, two of the greatest quartets in the business were scheduled to appear at this particular show in Pensacola: James Blackwood and the Blackwood Brothers and the Statesmen, featuring Jake Hess as lead singer and the famous Jim "Big Chief" Wetherington, their flashy bass singer. Some of my friends were going and encouraged me to come with them, so I bought a ticket. The singers on the program were some of the very people I loved to listen to on the radio; I had recordings of many of them. To an impressionable nineteen-year-old who felt both the call to ministry and the abiding love of music, these people were larger than life. They had recording contracts; they were traveling and singing in front of adoring fans; they spent their lives doing exactly what I was convinced I was supposed to do. To actually be in the same building with them was an opportunity I could hardly imagine.

The atmosphere at a gospel music show combines the fervor of a tent revival with the exuberance of a rock concert. The audience members are there to see and hear their favorite groups. Like me, many of them listened to records and radio shows featuring these very artists. As the evening progresses and the appearance of the more famous quartets nears, the excitement builds. Each group tries to outdo the last in capturing and holding the audience's attention, and with every set the air becomes more and more charged with anticipation.

The Blackwood Brothers came onstage to peals of applause and cheering, and they gave an amazing performance, combining arrangements of hymns familiar to the entire audience with exciting, new compositions calculated to grab hold of listeners' emotions and not let go.

The Blackwoods were followed by the Statesmen, and I'll never forget, as long as I live, the impression they made on me as they came onstage: They all had pencil-thin mustaches and they wore matching suits of shiny, black mohair. Their bold, black-and-white-striped ties stood out starkly against their crisp, white shirts, and the black-and-white wingtip shoes they all wore made their footwork almost as interesting as what they did with their voices.

The setup was typically simple: two microphones for the singers to share, and a miked piano for the keyboard man. If the pianist also sang or MC'ed for the group, there would be a microphone by the keyboard. Hovie Lister was the pianist for the Statesmen, and he did his part to whip the crowd into a near-frenzy as they closed their performance with a snappy, up-tempo song called "Get Away, Jordan." It featured some choreography on the chorus: a quick, coordinated backstep when they sang the tag line, "Get away, Jordan . . ." The singers would do tricks with the microphones, tilting and moving them back and forth as each singer had a solo line or a lead phrase. Big Chief wowed the crowd with his frenetic movement, shaking his leg and moving his shoulders in time with the music. Hovie Lister, I remember, actually leaped down onto the floor at one point, shouting at the audience through his microphone. As I said, it was a little like going to a revival service and a little like attending a show by—well, by Elvis Presley. By the end of the night, I was convinced beyond all doubt my destiny was to become a gospel music performer just like the Blackwoods and the Statesmen.

Over the next few years, I began to seek out opportunities to connect with other gospel musicians. Gradually, I began having chances to perform. In 1960, I landed my first professional gig as pianist with an Atlanta-based group called the Harmoneers.

I was the executive producer of the documentary He Touched Me: The Gospel Music of Elvis Presley. *In an interview for that project, Terry Blackwood explained: "The quartets would make the circuit. . . . There were several southern towns that would take a concert every month. . . . There'd be 5,000 people every month to come to a concert."*

When I joined the Harmoneers, I became part of a culture and a lifestyle that was rewarding, but also difficult. True, gospel music captured my imagination and I was dedicated to using my talents to the best of my ability, but the life was not an easy one.

A handful of promoters booked the large shows in the main cities on the circuit: Wally Fowler took care of Nashville, Atlanta, and Birmingham; W. B. Nowlin booked weekend dates in Texas; Lloyd Orrell worked in Chicago, Detroit, and Grand Rapids; and Sonny Simmons' territory was around Cleveland, Cincinnati, and Louisville. There were promoters who worked the West Coast, and one or two in Canada. Along with the other professional groups, we were booked for all-night sings a couple of times a year at each of these venues. In between these "major" events, we tried to book "fill-in" dates in the churches, schools, and various community halls of the smaller towns along the way.

For a lesser-known group like ours, a typical road trip might originate with an invitation from a promoter to appear at an all-night singing in one of the cities on the circuit—Little Rock, Arkansas, let's say. It's about five hundred miles from Atlanta to Little Rock, and, of course, in 1960 there were no interstate highways. We would try to schedule appearances in churches, schools, or anywhere else along the way we could gather enough people to pay a quarter each to come and listen to us. At each performance, we'd offer our records for sale, trying to build our listener base. So, after singing for an hour or two and hawking records or signing souvenir eight-by-ten glossies at a church in some tank town, the five of us would start loading up.

We'd pack our records and our small sound system into the trunk of our car, which was usually a Cadillac with big tail fins—we had a certain image to maintain, after all—dress in our comfortable traveling clothes, and carefully lay out our suits and ties atop the gear in the trunk. We might drive three or four hours, or even all night, alternating drivers in two-hour shifts, depending on how much road we needed to cover to get to our next engagement. When we arrived, we usually got a "cleanup room" at a local motel and changed into our suits and ties. If we didn't have time for a cleanup room, we'd go straight to the performance location and change in a classroom, locker room, or whatever was available. Sometimes I felt as if I needed to scrape the film of sleep out of my eyes or the road grime off my teeth, but we did what we needed to do to freshen up and get ready for the next performance.

We did this for as many as three hundred days out of the year. We sacrificed what most people would consider a normal lifestyle—going home in the evening to wives and children, for example—to pursue our dream. We also viewed our work as ministry, believing that God had planted in us the desire and talent to take the gospel message in song to the people who came to hear us. We worked hard to make that dream a reality. If the travel schedule sounds grueling, that's because it was.

Incidentally, the grind of the constant road time led directly to an innovation that has become a standard feature of the entertainment lifestyle: the tour bus. J. D. Sumner, the bass singer who replaced Bill Lyles with the Blackwoods and later became one of Elvis' mentors, grew weary of folding his lanky, six-foot-five-inch frame into an automobile for the trip to the next engagement. When he joined the Blackwood Brothers Quartet, he persuaded them to purchase a used passenger bus for $5,000. They ripped out all the seats and installed five recliners in the front section, one for each man to ride and sleep in. In the rear and lower compartments of the coach, they had plenty of storage space for equipment, records, sheet music, and clothing. This idea caught on rapidly, and soon the major quartets all had their own customized coaches in which they could travel the circuit in relative comfort.

Today, the customized-coach industry has become indispensable to entertainers, sports figures, and even politicians. It has also become a little more expensive: the shell alone can cost upwards of $300,000, and the complete build-out of the inside often runs another $700,000 or so. But it all started with J. D. Sumner and his need for more leg room.

From what I've been able to learn, my beginnings had much in common with Elvis', even though he was born in Tupelo, Mississippi, a long way from Albany, New York. Gospel music was the first music he ever knew, and, like him, I grew up in a churchgoing, Bible-believing family. Is it any wonder, then, that the same music that so captured his imagination would captivate mine as well? How and why did this happen to two young guys from such different cultural and geographical backgrounds? As I've pondered that question, I can only conclude that for whatever reason, Elvis Presley and I shared one thing above all others: a deep love for gospel music.

As many people know, Elvis Aaron Presley was born to Vernon and Gladys Presley in Tupelo, Mississippi, on January 8, 1935. He was the surviving twin; his brother, Jesse Garon, was stillborn. His parents brought him home to a two-room house barely four hundred square feet in size. His circumstances could hardly have been more humble, but he would remember and appreciate all his life the love he received from his family. His father was a hardworking man who stayed with his son throughout his life, supporting the pursuit of his dreams and, in later years, assisting with the financial oversight of his son's interests.

But it was with his mother that Elvis developed the deepest and most lasting of bonds. She kept constant watch over her son, walking him to and from school each day, even into his teenage years. He would never forget her devotion and her constancy. In many important ways, Gladys Presley's presence would make itself known throughout Elvis' life, often at moments when he was searching for guidance.

The Presleys were known to their Tupelo neighbors as a musical family. One of Elvis' earliest gifts was a guitar, purchased from a local hardware store. Residents of the small Mississippi town recall the Presleys sitting on the front porch of their small house in the evenings, singing. Sometimes, one or more of Elvis' uncles or aunts would come over and join in passing the time with music. Of course, no one in Tupelo at that time suspected they were listening to a voice that would become one of the most distinctive, well-known voices in American musical history.

The Presleys attended the First Assembly of God Church in East Tupelo, pastored by Reverend James Ballard, and later the First Assembly of God of Tupelo, where Reverend Rex Dyson was the minister; the three Presleys were baptized as members of this congregation. Gladys Presley would report that even as a toddler Elvis would squirm out of her lap and run down to the front of the church where the choir stood, watching them and imitating their voices and movements. A fifth-grade teacher once related that Elvis spontaneously demonstrated his musical talents, breaking into his own rendition of a then-popular song, "Old Shep." With her encouragement, he would repeat his performance for a talent contest at a state fair.

Picture this scene: Elvis Presley, probably no more than eight or ten years old, sits in the pews of the Assembly of God Church on a hot summer night in Tupelo. The windows of the church are open, and the women are working those cardboard funeral-home fans for all they're worth. Elvis is squirming in his seat with excitement, because he has come, with his mom and dad, to a gospel singing by a real quartet, and he can hardly wait for the show to start. He has heard this quartet sing on the radio, and he can hardly believe he's about to see them in person.

A former neighbor, Janelle McComb, *relates her memory of this squirmy kid: "We'd see him around town, see him at gospel singings, but . . . remember, back in those days, [we] weren't talking about the Elvis Presley that you see now. . . . That was Gladys and Vernon's kid."*

Most likely, the group got into town that morning, on their way to or from an all-night singing in Memphis. They went to the local radio station, a 500-watt setup broadcasting only during the daytime and barely reaching the city limits, and made a special pitch for tonight's performance at the church, telling everyone to be sure to attend, and "bring a friend." During the rest of the day, they set up their record racks in the church vestibule, re-arranged the podium furniture, hefted the massive upright piano onto the platform, and went somewhere to rest for a little while, clean up, and change into their concert attire.

Finally, when Elvis thinks he can't wait another second, the preacher steps up on the podium. He welcomes everyone and, with the accompanist's help, leads the crowd in a few songs to get things started. Elvis sings out in his clear, child's voice, along with his mother and dad and everyone else. And then it's time for the main event.

"I'd like y'all to welcome these boys," the preacher says, nodding toward the five men sitting in the front pew, smiling and looking perfectly relaxed in their matching suits and ties.

"They're going to do some of your favorite songs, and so I'm fixing to turn 'em loose on you now. Boys, get on up here."

The quartet takes the stage. Elvis drinks in the sight of them. Their hair is perfectly combed and the white handkerchiefs in the breast pockets of their coats look as clean and crisp as a brand-new dollar bill. The piano player sits down and launches into a lively intro, his left hand loping up and down in octaves and his right hand banging out the chords. Elvis quickly recognizes the tune: "Jesus, Hold My Hand." The four singers are animated, smiling and gesturing to the crowd. Elvis feels as if they're singing every word just for him.

After they've sung for about a half hour or so, the quartet takes a break and the preacher comes back. "Now, folks, these boys agreed to come here and sing for whatever we'd give them, so right now we want to let them take a break while we take up a love offering. Gas is expensive, folks—up to fifteen cents a gallon, the other day—so let's all do our part and help these boys out so they can keep on spreading the Gospel in song."

To young Elvis, these performers were heroes—his idols. In his young imagination, he could see himself standing onstage in a crisp, tailored suit, singing the songs he knew so well, entertaining people and living the life of a professional gospel singer. It was the first dream of his life, and one he never fully left.

IN THE FALL OF 1948, seeking better employment opportunities, Vernon Presley moved his family a little over a hundred miles northwest to Memphis, a city rapidly consolidating its position as one of the leading cities of the South. Memphis was a musical hotbed as well, pulsing with the energy of the emerging

"Memphis Sound." In addition to the rise of rhythm and blues, gospel music—both the white, Southern gospel variety and the African American style, highly influenced by the folk spiritual tradition—staked a firm claim on the Memphis musical scene.

As a boy living in the housing projects near downtown Memphis, Elvis would have heard much of the music of the streets. Lauderdale Courts, a primarily African American neighborhood, was near his home. He is said to have spent time playing his guitar and singing with the kids in the neighborhood.

Elvis was also known to attend African American churches where, from the balcony, he would observe and absorb the music and movements of the choirs and individual performers. Reverend Herbert Brewster, pastor of the East Trigg Baptist Church, an African American congregation, shared that Elvis was part of the group of musicians he encouraged.

My good friend Sherman Andrus, a member of The Imperials in the 1970s and one of the first African American performers in a Southern gospel group, attested to his amazement at Elvis' deep knowledge of African American gospel music. "I think his knowledge was even more extensive than mine," Andrus said. "I prided myself on knowing all that stuff. And man, we'd be hanging out and he'd be talking about singers that I didn't even know about." Other musicians often noted the breadth of Elvis' personal collection of African American gospel recordings. He had everybody's records: the Harmonizing Four, the Golden Gate Quartet, and those by lesser-known black gospel groups. He listened to them for hours and hours, and it greatly influenced his singing style and approach.

Elvis' earliest-stated and most frequently repeated ambition was to become a gospel singer. He also wanted to learn to play the piano well enough to accompany a quartet, or perhaps a church choir. Though he would never receive formal training or lessons, his ability to play "by ear" and to analyze and comprehend the chord structure and voicing of harmonic singing would amaze those of us who worked with him in later years.

Elvis could hardly have been in a more favorable location to foster his gospel ambitions. He lived two blocks from Ellis Auditorium, the venue for the National Quartet Convention, a Southern gospel quartet extravaganza that drew the leading quartets to Memphis for concerts attended faithfully by thousands.

In the early 1950s, Southern gospel quartets had such established popularity that the performances on the circuit would frequently sell out auditoriums seating 5,000 people or more. One of the biggest shows, however, was the National Quartet Convention. When the convention was in town each year, Elvis, who had scratched and saved to purchase a ticket, would attend and listen to the gospel music he loved. He became familiar to the members of the leading quartets, including J. D. Sumner, who performed with the Blackwoods at that time and was known as the "lowest bass singer in the world." Elvis especially loved the deep, sonorous tones of the bass singers and the characteristic way they would boom out the short lead phrases that gave Southern gospel choruses their punch.

Ellis Auditorium was also the location for shows by leading quartets such as the Statesmen from Atlanta, and especially the Blackwood Brothers, who were from Memphis and often promoted singing events featuring themselves and other groups. On one occasion, J. D. Sumner noticed that the young boy who had been attending the sings so faithfully was absent. Then, the next time, he was back. When he had the opportunity to speak to Elvis, J.D. asked him where he was at the last concert and why he hadn't attended. Elvis replied that he didn't have enough money for a ticket. J.D. told him he wouldn't need any money from that point on. "You just come to the stage door and I'll let you in for nothing." And that's the way it remained. Later, J.D. said, "About the next thing I knew he was letting me in *his* stage door." It was the beginning of one of the most enduring friendships of Elvis Presley's life.

James Blackwood recalls, "We had gospel concerts at the downtown Ellis Auditorium during those years, and Elvis would always come."

The Statesmen and the Blackwood Brothers, as the dominant Southern gospel quartets of the day, became young Elvis Presley's idols—just as they became mine. Elvis credited the Blackwood Brothers and the Statesmen for much of his early inspiration, and comparisons are frequently made between his singing style and that of Jake Hess, the lead singer for the Statesmen. Much of Elvis' phrasing, articulation, and vocal projection are reminiscent of Jake. It has even been suggested that Elvis' body movements resembled those of "Big Chief" Wetherington, the Statesmen's famous leg-twitching bass singer. It's also worth noting that the Statesmen, with their distinctive long, black, combed-back hairstyles, may even have had some influence on Elvis' look, especially during his early days.

In 1954, Elvis received a musical setback that would, in retrospect, be seen as helping to set him on the path of destiny. The

Songfellows was a group formed under the sponsorship of the influential Blackwood Brothers Quartet, a sort of "farm team" for up-and-coming young singers. A vacancy existed due to the death of R. W. Blackwood, who was killed in the crash of their private plane, along with fellow quartet member bass singer Bill Lyles (subsequently replaced by J. D. Sumner). Cecil Blackwood was "called up" from the Songfellows to take his brother's place in the Blackwood Brothers Quartet. Auditions were held at a Memphis auditorium to find Cecil's replacement. Elvis, of course, auditioned.

In the meantime, he wandered into the Sun Records studios on Union Avenue and made an acetate recording of two songs, "My Happiness" and "That's When Your Heartaches Begin." The evidence concerning Elvis' motivation for making the recordings is somewhat clouded; tradition has asserted that the record was to be a birthday gift for his mother. However, since the session was conducted in the summer of 1953, well after Gladys' April birthday, some have suggested that Elvis was using his mother's "birthday gift" as an excuse to audition for Sam Phillips, the owner of Sun Records. About a year later, Elvis would sign his first recording contract and be on his way to becoming an American superstar. At any rate, Elvis was unable to take the job with the Songfellows because he decided to pursue a solo recording career. What might have happened if the timing had been different, and Elvis had instead cast his lot with a professional gospel group? We can only wonder.

We do know, however, that despite Elvis' recording successes, the sound of gospel music was still ringing in his ears. In 1954, Elvis paid a backstage visit to the popular group the Jordanaires, who were appearing at the Mid-South Cotton Carnival as a backup group for Eddy Arnold. The first Southern gospel group to adapt the rhythms and syncopations characteristic of African American gospel, the Jordanaires had a unique sound and were widely respected in the Southern gospel world, though not regulars on the circuit due to their recording commitments. In the 1950s and 1960s they made numerous appearances onstage as backup singers for solo performers, as well as being frequently in demand for studio work for such stars as Brenda Lee, Jim Reeves, Marty Robbins, and Patsy Cline. Perhaps most significantly, they were at the time the only Southern gospel group to have a contract with Columbia Records; the Blackwoods and the Statesmen recorded on the RCA Victor label.

Reportedly, Elvis told the group during his conversation with them that he admired their sound and desired to record and perform with them. "If I can ever afford it," he said, "I want to work with you guys." As time would prove, Elvis made good on this wish.

Later, Elvis would perform on *The Louisiana Hayride*, a popular radio show of the time some have called "the junior *Grand Ole Opry*." Also appearing on the bill, though not as backup for Elvis, were the Jordanaires. Thus, when the time came and Elvis "could afford it," he and the Jordanaires were no strangers to each other. Because of their unique style and the way they were almost universally admired in the industry, many—in the Southern gospel world, certainly—thought it was only right, in retrospect, that Elvis should have chosen the Jordanaires to support him on his rapid rise to fame. They would make their first recording together in July 1956.

During this time, a phenomenon was developing that would come to be known as "Elvismania." With the 1956 release of the hit single "Heartbreak Hotel" by Elvis' new label, RCA Victor, followed by his national television debut on the Dorsey Brothers' *Stage Show*, Elvis was quickly becoming a household name. Unfortunately, not all mentions of his name were kind.

The newspapers and other media reported he was vulgar, and such characterizations really hurt Elvis. He said on one occasion, "That's the farthest thing from my mind. I wouldn't do anything . . . that my mother would see on T.V. that might be classed as vulgar." To Elvis' dismay, he was becoming the personification of everything wrong with the rapidly developing musical style known as rock and roll. Preachers across the country denounced Elvis Presley by name from their pulpits. On occasion, he was even scrutinized by local law enforcement authorities to make certain he wasn't committing some sort of public lewdness, even to the reported extent of filming his shows for possible evidence. Elvis' appearances on the *Ed Sullivan Show* generated such a storm of protest from certain viewers the show's producers made the decision to keep the camera focused on the area above Elvis' waist. But in his third—and final—appearance on the show in 1957, Elvis made a demand that those who complained about the vulgarity of "Elvis the Pelvis" would hardly have expected: He wanted to sing a gospel song.

"Peace in the Valley" was one of his mother's favorite songs. For his last performance on the *Ed Sullivan Show*, the network didn't want a gospel song. However, Elvis said, "No, I told my mother that I was going to do 'Peace in the Valley' for her, and I'm going to do it."

And he did. Backed by the Jordanaires, Elvis delivered a heartfelt performance of this gospel standard to a nationwide audience, a famous, often-viewed segment, even though it was during television's early black-and-white days. Sullivan, seeming uncomfortable during his introduction of the performance, referred to Elvis' wish to create a certain "mood." Though Ed Sullivan and television network officials may have been uncomfortable with seeing and hearing "Peace in the Valley" going out over their airwaves, public reaction would soon prove that the public was far more accepting of this new, gospel side of Elvis than industry professionals could have anticipated.

The response to Elvis' television performance was immediate—and enthusiastic. RCA, hoping to capitalize on the excitement Elvis created, decided to record a four-song record that included "Peace in the Valley." It was a huge success that led eventually to Elvis recording an entire album of gospel songs.

It is perhaps fitting that Elvis' love of gospel was first brought to the public's attention by his wish to honor his mother. There can be no question Gladys Presley loved intensely the image of her treasured son on the television screen, singing one of her favorite songs. It may have been the crowning moment of her life, for on August 14, 1958, Gladys Presley died in a Memphis hospital from a heart attack.

Chapter Two

THE MAKING OF A SUPERSTAR

Elvis was crushed by his mother's death. He arranged for a chartered aircraft to bring the Blackwood Brothers, his mother's favorite gospel quartet, to Memphis to sing for her funeral. Having recently been inducted into the U.S. Army, Elvis was forced into lengthy negotiations involving reams of red tape to be able to attend his mother's service. He received a special dispensation, however, and upon his arrival in Memphis, James Blackwood remembers Elvis going over to the casket, kissing his mother, and saying, "Mama, I'd give every dime I have and go back to digging ditches, just to have you back." Gordon Stoker of the Jordanaires said in an interview that to this day, when he visits Graceland, he can still see Elvis in his mind's eye, sitting on the third step of the staircase that leads up to the bedrooms, weeping uncontrollably.

Gordon Stoker recalls, "The lowest point in Elvis' life was when his mother died."

Years later, in his Las Vegas shows and elsewhere, Elvis would perform the haunting ballad "I'll Remember You." It's not too difficult at all to imagine, as he sang the words:

I'll be lonely / oh, so lonely;
Living only to remember you

the face he thought of was the doting mother who held him in her lap at church and walked him to school.

Elvis was inducted into the U.S. Army the previous spring. The month after his mother's death, he was assigned to an armored division stationed in Germany. He requested and received a deferment to permit him to complete the filming of his fourth movie, *King Creole*. Thanks to the strategic management of "Colonel Tom" Parker, the movies Elvis would make in the 1950s and 1960s not only made him one of the most recognizable stars in the nation, they also guaranteed the wide distribution of his recordings. Little did Elvis' fans know that not only during his army hitch, but for a total of nine years, until 1968, if you wanted to see Elvis you had to go to the movies; Colonel Parker worded Elvis' contracts so he was not supposed to make any live appearances until his obligations to the movie studios were fulfilled. Elvis would become more and more impatient with this restriction, but because of the deep respect he held for the Colonel, he did his best to abide by the limitations the contracts imposed.

During his time in the army, Elvis was, by all reports, a model soldier, receiving the commendation of his superiors for his performance during maneuvers. Rumors surfaced in the media, however, about his romantic pursuits when he was off duty. While he was in Germany he also met the woman who would capture his heart: young Priscilla Beaulieu, the daughter of an air force officer. Elvis' close associates at the time noted there was something profoundly different in his attitude toward Priscilla than he customarily displayed with the many other women in his orbit. Clearly, there was something special about her. He opened himself up to her in a way he rarely had with anyone else—even the close friends who lived with him and his father in Germany. Though she was only fourteen when they met, Elvis never forgot her.

Because of his independent financial means, Elvis was able to rent a house near the base, and he reportedly spent a great deal of time singing and listening to gospel favorites from the large record collection he brought to Germany with him. Charlie Hodge, a performer in his own right whom Elvis met on the troop ship taking them both across the Atlantic, lived with Elvis in Germany and may have been instrumental in sharing his interest in such groups as the original Jordanaires with the Matthews Brothers. In all likelihood, their shared interest in gospel music drew them closer as friends. During a leave in Paris, Elvis attended a show by the Golden Gate Quartet, a black gospel group with heavy influences on both Elvis and the Jordanaires, and went backstage after the show. He reportedly sang gospel songs for hours with the group, including some songs not familiar to the Golden Gate Quartet.

Another discovery Elvis made during his time in Germany— one that would have dire implications in years to come—was the use of "uppers." This is a difficult topic for me to approach; because of the respect and friendship I enjoyed with Elvis, I don't like discussing negative subjects. However, Elvis' use of pharmaceuticals has been widely reported in many different settings, and I have reluctantly concluded over a period of years that the issue is not really open to doubt. At the same time, though, I can honestly say during my time performing with Elvis, I never personally witnessed him taking pills, nor was drug use any part of our time together, either onstage or off. If he became addicted, it was a slow process that could have begun during his army days and gradually reached a point where his judgment in the matter was clouded. But I'm very certain Elvis didn't try to force it on anybody, in my experience.

Apparently, soldiers in the field would sometimes take stimulants such as amphetamines to maintain energy and alertness when adequate sleep was difficult to get. Elvis became a user of these pills, and though he tried to exercise caution, he apparently saw nothing wrong or problematic with this. He regarded uppers as being in much the same category as aspirin: something you took if you needed it, and not at all like "bad" drugs such as cocaine and heroin. This was just one of the contradictions in Elvis' very complicated life that worried those of us who admired him and wished him well.

Upon the completion of Elvis' army service, the first order of business was resuming the successful series of movies for which he was under contract. His popularity had not faded at all during his time in the service, even though he adhered to the agreement not to record or perform at all during his tour of duty. Colonel Parker carefully orchestrated the gradual release of songs recorded by Elvis for RCA before leaving for his tour of duty, and despite RCA's protests, the strategy proved successful—it was one of the many instances confirming the confidence in the Colonel's management Elvis consistently professed. The movies were eagerly anticipated by the public, and each movie's release was accompanied by the release of the sound-track album; most of the albums reached the top of the sales charts.

But even during the recording of the sound-track albums, Elvis had gospel music on his mind. At one point, we're told, the label executives became impatient with Elvis' habit of sitting down at the piano and gathering the quartet around him to sing gospel songs.

During rehearsals for *Jailhouse Rock*, for example, Elvis was in the habit of showing up on the set and finding the nearest piano. Before doing anything else, he'd sit down and start playing, and pretty soon he'd be singing gospel songs with the Jordanaires, who were there with him at the time. Studio executives, of course, were very mindful of the amount of time being spent in what they viewed as unproductive pursuits; they watched the clock and, no doubt, calculated minute by minute how much money it was costing them for Elvis to sing gospel instead of rehearsing or filming the next scene.

At one point, the director instructed the Jordanaires to refrain from singing with Elvis: "When Elvis comes back after dinner, don't go over and sing with him again; we want to get busy. If he starts singing a spiritual, don't sing, don't do a thing. This is costing us a lot of money. We've got to get this next scene finished, and we don't want him wasting our time and our money."

When Elvis returned to the studio after the break, he sat down at the piano and began singing a gospel song, as was his custom. Soon, though, he noticed the Jordanaires were holding back from joining in the song. When he asked about their silence, the quartet informed him, perhaps somewhat sheepishly, that the studio executives requested they not encourage Elvis to sing gospel songs, since the meter was running.

Elvis immediately let it be known that he would sing gospel if he so desired. "Listen, if I want to sit here and sing these gospel songs all week long, I'll do it. I'll know when I'm ready to work," he reportedly said. And then he walked out of the studio, leaving behind a group of puzzled executives, as well as the Colonel and his entire entourage. Some who were there do remember, however, to Elvis' credit, that the next morning he reported promptly at the nine-o'clock call time ready to go to work.

Sometimes, though, Elvis was actually able to combine moviemaking and gospel music, as in the tent-revival scene in *The Trouble with Girls.* In this lively footage, Elvis is seen at the front of the congregation with studio singers the Men of Song as his backup—the ensemble billed in the movie as "the Bible Singers"—delivering a jumping rendition of "Swing Down, Sweet Chariot." Still, those near him remember that Elvis, for the most part, merely endured the recording of the songs for the movies, many of which he performed only to fulfill his obligations.

In fact, Elvis was very conscientious about fulfilling his obligations—to his record company, to the movie studios, and certainly to his public. One near-constant theme in his interviews throughout his career is his appreciation for his public and his wish to give them the very best he had to offer. Time and again, those whom he worked with on the movie set and in the recording studio—co-stars, producers, directors, engineers, and fellow musicians—have said Elvis was almost unfailingly polite and respectful, not to mention punctilious about arriving when he was supposed to and not leaving until the job was finished. Only rarely, especially as the long process of fulfilling his movie contracts wore on toward its end and his patience with the inferior material—as he perceived it—began to thin, did anyone see Elvis project anything less than a professional and courteous attitude toward those with whom he was working.

Even though his movies were quickly making him rich and famous, gospel music was never far from Elvis' mind. Photos of the period show him in the company of such gospel greats as Mahalia Jackson. Always a fan, he was a voracious collector of albums by singers like Jackson, the Staple Singers, and the Clara Ward Singers. He also continued his regular attendance at the National Quartet Convention in Memphis.

Tony Brown of the Stamps relates that "he always showed up every year. And now, looking back on it, it's because he wanted to be part of it. That was important to him."

Inevitably, Elvis' appearances backstage at the convention would cause quite a stir. There was electricity in the air when those of us in attendance heard he was coming. We'd wait, and he would enter the room, and the excitement backstage was thick—even before the people in the audience knew he was there. When Elvis walked in, it was like royalty had entered the room: everybody stopped. We were in awe, because few of us had ever met anybody like him.

Like almost everyone who was at the Quartet Convention in those days, I also have an "Elvis story." In 1961, I was still playing piano for the Harmoneers, a group of older singers from Atlanta. We were scheduled for several performances during the convention that year, some falling early in the evening and some late at night. The Harmoneers were certainly not headliners; we were just one of the more than fifty quartets performing at the convention. On one of the nights we had an earlier performance, and a rumor was buzzing around the backstage area that Elvis Presley would be making an appearance later in the evening—not to perform, of course, but to hear the Statesmen or one of his other favorite groups. In fact, J. D. Sumner was directing the convention that year, and it's likely that he personally contacted his former protégé. I remember that, late in the evening when Elvis finally showed up (in time for the Statesmen, the Blackwood Brothers, or one of his other favorite groups, no doubt), I was standing about twenty feet from him as he was surrounded by admirers. I was completely in awe of this larger-than-life figure actually standing so close to me.

I waited for an opening, and though I was a nervous wreck, I walked up to him, rehearsing in my mind what I would say: *I'm Joe Moscheo . . . my mother is a devoted fan of yours. . . . Could I please have your autograph?*

He looked at me and never missed a beat. Probably sensing my nervousness, before I could speak, Elvis said, "I know who you are. You're the piano player for the Harmoneers, right?"

"Yes, sir," I said, even though he was only two years my senior. I stammered out something about my mother and an autograph.

He smiled his famous crooked smile. "Sure. I'll exchange with you."

I was flabbergasted. Elvis Presley was actually asking to swap autographs with me. To this day, I vividly remember how flattered I was that he would bother to attempt putting me at ease. That sort of unassuming charm was one reason for the hold he

had on people: He could speak to you and look at you and make you feel you were the only person in the world he was interested in at that moment. True, he could also be impatient, arbitrary, and jealous of any attention paid to someone else. He wasn't perfect. But more often than not, he was polite, gracious, and far more humble than you'd expect given his fame and reputation. Before I met him, I was an admirer. After I met him that night in Memphis, I was a fan.

As I look back on it, it boggles my mind to consider how eager we were; just hoping to get a glimpse of Elvis Presley. And then actually to have a chance to meet him and speak to him. At the time, I couldn't imagine anything bigger happening in my life. A few years later, when the phone call came inviting me to work with him, I can't possibly describe the amazement I felt and continue to feel, even to this day.

Jake Hess, Elvis' favorite lead singer, was the founding leader of The Imperials, but at that time he was with the Statesmen. He tells how sometimes, while performing, he would feel a tap on his shoulder. He would look over to see Elvis, who sang the same vocal part as Hess, motioning him toward the wings so he could take Hess's place onstage. Hess said, "Everybody would ask me, 'How was it to sing with Elvis?' I never did get to sing with him in those days, in the Statesmen days. He would sing my part, and I would watch and listen."

By the way, some readers many not realize that when he formed his "all-star" group in the 1960s and was trying to come up with a name for it, Hess went back to the name of a quartet that sang on the radio in the Dallas–Fort Worth area in the 1950s. As the stars of an early-morning show sponsored by the Imperial Sugar Company, the Imperial Quartet became quite popular during this period. Jake liked the name, and when he put our group together we became The Imperials.

James Blackwood remembers that in the earlier years at the convention, Elvis would come onstage and sing, usually "Peace in the Valley," and the Blackwoods would back him up. And then, after several years at the convention, Elvis said, "Just introduce me and I'll come out and wave to the audience. Colonel doesn't want me performing."

Indeed, Elvis' manager was reluctant to allow his "boy" to sing in public, believing live performances would dilute the public's desire to buy tickets at the box office. After several years, the Colonel put his foot down: "No free singing" became his motto. For this reason, Elvis gave no live performances of any kind from 1961 to 1968. He chafed at this restraint, longing to get back in front of the audiences that filled him with energy and perform the music he loved. The only exceptions to the Colonel's rule were a charity concert Elvis gave in Memphis in February of 1961 for the benefit of local causes and his Elvis Presley Youth Center in Tupelo and, a month or so later, his USS *Arizona* Memorial benefit concert in Hawaii, staged just before he began the filming of *Blue Hawaii*. The Colonel had a method to his madness, even in these two situations: he was eager for the positive public-relations opportunities connected with such benevolence on the part of his boy, and indeed, though a good deal of money was raised, the Colonel saw to it that the PR value of the events was maximized.

AT THE FAMOUS "Million Dollar Session," an impromptu gathering with Johnny Cash, Jerry Lee Lewis, and Carl Perkins at

1. *The Statesmen Quartet: l. to r.: Denver Crumpler, Jake Hess, Doy Ott, Jim "Big Chief" Wetherington, Hovie Lister (front).* GAITHER ARCHIVES

2. *The Blackwood Brothers, circa 1954: l. to r.: James Blackwood (lead singer), R. W. Blackwood (baritone), Jackie Marshall (piano player), Bill Shaw (tenor), Bill Lyles (bass).* GAITHER ARCHIVES

3. *The Harmoneers: l. to r.: (back row) Joe Moscheo, Bob Crews, Seal "Low Note" Hilton; (front row) Happy Edwards and Jimi Hall.* JOE MOSCHEO PERSONAL COLLECTION

4. *Joe onstage: with the Harmoneers at an All-Night Singing in Atlanta, Ga., 1960.* JOE MOSCHEO PERSONAL COLLECTION

5. *The Blackwood Brothers: l. to r.: Bill Shaw, James Blackwood, Cecil Blackwood, J. D. Sumner, and Jackie Marshall.* Gaither Archives

6. *J. D. Sumner and the Stamps, circa mid-1960s: l. to r.: (back row) Duke Dumas (guitar), Tony Brown (piano), Donnie Sumner (lead singer), Mylon LeFevre (bass player); (front row) Jim Hill (tenor), J. D. (bass singer), Jimmy Blackwood (baritone).*
Gaither Archives

7. *The Jordanaires, 1952, (from l): first tenor Bill Matthews, baritone and arranger Monty Matthews, bass Culley Holt, pianist and tenor Gordon Stoker, and second tenor Bobby Hubbard.* Gaither Archives

8. *Backstage at the Quartet Convention in Memphis, circa 1955: l. to r.: James Blackwood, Jackie Marshall, J. D. Sumner, Elvis Presley, and R. W. Blackwood, Jr.* http://www.biwa. ne.jp/~presley/

9. *Record jacket of The Imperials with Jake Hess, 1965: Gary McSpadden, Armond Morales, Joe Moscheo, Jim Murray, Jake Hess.* JOE MOSCHEO PERSONAL COLLECTION

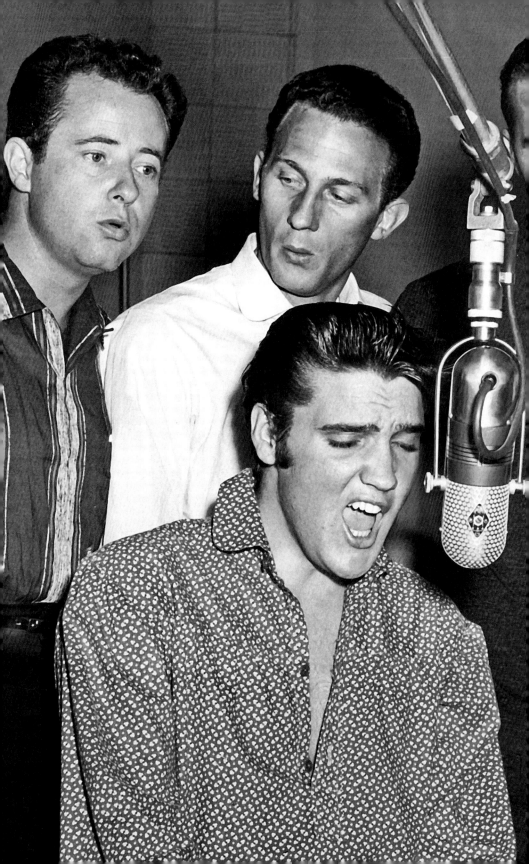

10. The Jordanaires backing Elvis Presley in the studio: l. to r.: (back row) Gordon Stoker, Hoyt Hawkins, Neal Mathews, and Hugh Cherry. Elvis at piano.

11. His Hand in Mine *album cover, recorded in 1960.* USED BY PERMISSION, © ELVIS PRESLEY ENTERPRISES, INC.

12. Elvis performing "If I Can Dream" for the '68 Special. Used by permission,
© Elvis Presley Enterprises, Inc.

13. Sheet music for "How Great Thou Art." Manna Music

14. How Great Thou Art *album cover.*

15. Elvis's Grammy for How Great Thou Art.

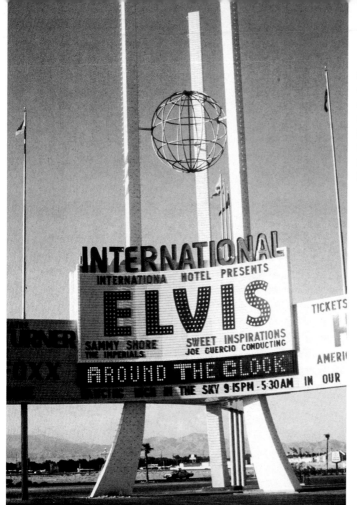

16. *Marquee in front of the International Hotel in Las Vegas announcing Elvis's 1969 appearance and giving proper credit to the other members of his show.* USED BY PERMISSION, © ELVIS PRESLEY ENTERPRISES, INC.

17. *The Imperials with Elvis Presley, 1969. One of the two groups backing Elvis when his show opened at the International Hotel.* JOE MOSCHEO PERSONAL COLLECTION

18. After-show gathering in Elvis's suite, 1972: Joe Moscheo at piano, with (l. to r.): Terry Blackwood, Sherman Andrus, Jim Murray, "Mama" Cass Elliot, Armond Morales, Marty Allen (comedian), Elvis Presley, Linda Thompson. PHOTO TAKEN BY WINNIE ANDRUS

19. The Sweet Inspirations, 1969: clockwise from left: Estelle Brown, Sylvia Shemwell, Cissy Houston, and Myrna Smith. USED BY PERMISSION, © ELVIS PRESLEY ENTERPRISES, INC.

20. Dove Award given to The Imperials for Best Male Group, 1969. Joe Moscheo PERSONAL COLLECTION

21. The Imperials with Dove Award in 1969: l. to r.: Terry Blackwood, Jim Murray, Joe Moscheo, Armond Morales, Roger Wiles. Joe Moscheo PERSONAL COLLECTION

22. *Joe Moscheo accepting Dove Award in 1969 for Best Male Group, given by the Gospel Music Association.* Joe Moscheo personal collection

23. *Elvis in rehearsal with cast for 1969 opening at the International Hotel.* USED BY PERMISSION, © ELVIS PRESLEY ENTERPRISES, INC.

24. *Elvis with The Imperials prior to show in front of their dressing room. International Hotel, Las Vegas, 1970.* JOE MOSCHEO PERSONAL COLLECTION

25. Elvis with The Imperials prior to a show, 1969. JOE MOSCHEO PERSONAL COLLECTION

26. Elvis with The Imperials backstage at the Landmark Hotel, Las Vegas, 1972: l. to r.: Joe Moscheo, Terry Blackwood, Jim Murray, Elvis Presley, Armond Morales, Larry Gatlin.
JOE MOSCHEO PERSONAL COLLECTION

Elvis
He Touched Me

HE TOUCHED ME ■ I GOT CONFIDENCE ■ AMAZING GRACE
SEEING IS BELIEVING ■ HE IS MY EVERYTHING ■ BOSOM OF ABRAHAM
AN EVENING PRAYER ■ LEAD ME, GUIDE ME ■ REACH OUT TO JESUS
THERE IS NO GOD BUT GOD ■ A THING CALLED LOVE ■ I JOHN

27. He Touched Me, *his Grammy Award–winning album.* USED BY PERMISSION, © ELVIS PRESLEY ENTERPRISES, INC.

28. Elvis Presley and Joe Moscheo, 1969. JOE MOSCHEO PERSONAL COLLECTION

29. Joe Moscheo and J. D. Sumner in front of Sumar Talent Agency, Nashville, Tenn., 1968. JOE MOSCHEO PERSONAL COLLECTION

30. The Imperials when Sherman Andrus first joined the group, 1972. Joe Moscheo PERSONAL COLLECTION

31. The Imperials ready for a network television appearance. Joe Moscheo PERSONAL COLLECTION

32. Personal note from Elvis after family tragedy. JOE MOSCHEO PERSONAL COLLECTION

33. The Imperials at the height of their popularity in Contemporary Christian Music. Joe Moscheo PERSONAL COLLECTION

34. The Stamps as they appeared with Elvis Presley: l. to r.: Bill Baize, Donnie Sumner, J. D. Sumner, Ed Enoch, Richard Sterban. GAITHER ARCHIVES

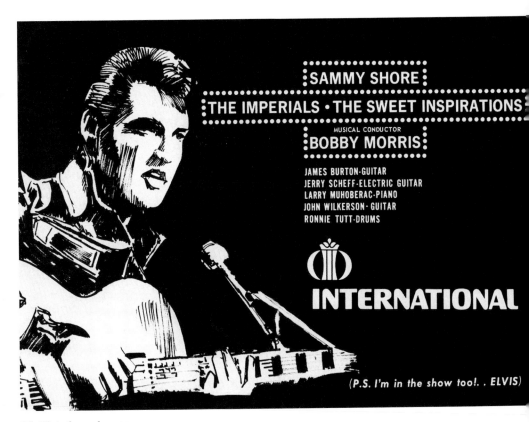

‡SAMMY SHORE‡

THE IMPERIALS • THE SWEET INSPIRATIONS

MUSICAL CONDUCTOR
‡BOBBY MORRIS‡

JAMES BURTON-GUITAR
JERRY SCHEFF-ELECTRIC GUITAR
LARRY MUHOBERAC-PIANO
JOHN WILKERSON-GUITAR
RONNIE TUTT-DRUMS

INTERNATIONAL

(P.S. I'm in the show too!. . ELVIS)

35. Elvis show ad. Joe Moscheo personal collection

36. The Stamps with Elvis: l. to r.: Bill Baize, Richard Sterban, Donnie Sumner, Elvis Presley, J. D. Sumner, Ed Enoch, Nick Bruno. Gaither Archives

37. *Full-page spread newspaper ad for Tahoe show. Note where Elvis's name appears in the billing.*

38. Joe Moscheo with Priscilla Presley at the 1976 Grammy Awards in Los Angeles. JOE MOSCHEO PERSONAL COLLECTION

39. Speech given by Joe at Elvis's induction into the Gospel Music Hall of Fame, 2001. JOE MOSCHEO

PERSONAL COLLECTION

Standing here, we represent a small part of the singers and musicians who worked with Elvis through the years, both in the studio and on personal appearances. We say thank you for that privilege and for exposing us and our music to an audience who might not have ever heard of gospel music. Thank you to the great Gordon Stoker and all the Jordanaires, Jake Hess and all the Imperials, to J.D. Sumner and all the Stamps Quartet Members and to all the Sweet Inspirations who always added so much to his personal appearances.

To us it seems fitting and proper that this has been accomplished. Elvis would be so proud of this honor. Elvis was a student and fan of gospel music. He loved it. He knew every word, every song, every songwriter, every arrangement. He knew each one of you by name and what part you sang, and could sing right along with you. His gospel music collection was quite extensive, and he would listen for hours to Monte and Bill Matthews, the Foggy River Boys, Jimmy Jones and the Harmonizing Four, The Golden Gate Quartet, The Blackwoods and Statesmen, the Bill Gaither Trio, and so many more. He admired you and respected you.

We would like to thank the Gospel Music Association, its Board of Directors, and the GMA Hall of Fame Committee for recognizing his contribution to gospel music and for bestowing this honor on our friend, Elvis Aaron Presley.

Sincerely

Joe Moscheo

11/27/01

Thanks Elvis

Special Elvis Souvenir Menu

Appetizers

Seafood Cocktail Supreme-Neptune   1.50
Supreme of Fresh Fruit au Kirsch   1.00
Fresh Chopped Chicken Livers   1.00

Salad

Hearts of Romaine with Crab Meat
Choice of Dressing

Entrees

Baked Lobster Tail - Internationale   15.00
Breast of Young Capon, Souvaroff, Wild Rice   15.00
Roast Prime Rib of Beef, au Jus   15.00
Broiled New York Steak, Maitre d'Hotel   15.00

Asparagus Tips en Butter   Parisienne Potatoes

Desserts

Assorted French Pastries   1.00   Parfait Internationale   1.00
Fresh Strawberry Tart, Chantilly   1.00
Assorted Ice Creams and Sherbet   .75

**Complete Elvis Souvenir Photo Album on Sale at
Hotel Entrance and Cafe Continental.**

40. Souvenir menu from the International Hotel. JOE MOSCHEO PERSONAL COLLECTION

FESTIVAL

Menu

Appetizers

Seafood Cocktail Supreme-Neptune   1.50
Supreme of Fresh Fruit au Kirsch   1.00
Fresh Chopped Chicken Livers   1.00

Salad

Hearts of Romaine with Crab Meat
Choice of Dressing

Entrees

Baked Lobster Tail - Internationale   15.00
Breast of Young Capon, Souvaroff, Wild Rice   15.00
Roast Prime Rib of Beef, au Jus   15.00
Broiled New York Steak, Maitre d'Hotel   15.00

Asparagus Tips en Butter   Parisienne Potatoes

Desserts

Chocolate Cake   1.00   Fresh Strawberry Tart, Chantilly   1.00
Cheese Cake with Fruit Topping   1.00
Assorted Ice Creams and Sherbet   .75

41. *Souvenir menu from the International Hotel.* Joe Moscheo personal collection

42. *Backstage passes for cast and crew from 1969 to 1971.* Joe Moscheo PERSONAL COLLECTION

43. *Award given to Imperials at induction into Gospel Music Hall of Fame.* JOE MOSCHEO PERSONAL COLLECTION

44. *The Imperials' certificate of induction into the Gospel Music Hall of Fame.* JOE MOSCHEO PERSONAL COLLECTION

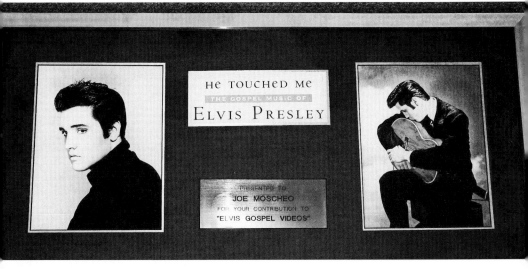

45. *Award presented to Joe Moscheo for production of* He Touched Me: The Gospel Music of Elvis Presley *DVD.* Joe Moscheo personal collection

46. *Award presented to Joe Moscheo for Gold video status of* He Touched Me: The Gospel Music of Elvis Presley *DVD.* Joe Moscheo personal collection

47. *The Imperials, present day: l. to r.: Terry Blackwood, Gus Gaches, Sherman Andrus, Joe Moscheo.*
USED BY PERMISSION OF THE IMPERIALS

48. *"All Access" memorabilia.*
JOE MOSCHEO PERSONAL COLLECTION

Sun Studios in Memphis in early December 1956, Elvis collaborated on a completely unrehearsed recording that would forever represent a special occasion in American popular music history. Elvis knew the guys were in the studio, and he dropped by to spend some time catching up on what was happening with their careers and their lives. Not surprisingly, considering four talented singers were gathered together in a place that encouraged musical creativity and spontaneity, Elvis eventually sat down at the piano and began noodling. Soon, the other guys gathered around and began to sing with him. All four of them shared similar backgrounds and influences, so it was natural that many of the songs in this spontaneous session were well-known gospel standards. The harmonies, the style, and the melodies of gospel music formed some of their earliest memories, and when the four of them started singing it was almost a given they'd end up singing gospel.

Among the songs captured on tape that day by the eager engineer were "Just a Little Talk with Jesus," "That Lonesome Valley," "I Shall Not Be Moved," "Peace in the Valley," "Down by the Riverside," "Farther Along," "Jesus Hold My Hand," and "On the Jericho Road."

This highly collectible recording went on to become one of the most famous and sought-after of all time. This illustrious group was composed of some of the best known and most beloved artists of our time. Carl Perkins would go on to write such hits as "Blue Suede Shoes" and "Daddy Sang Bass" (which was recorded by Johnny Cash in 1968 and quickly hit number one on the country charts). Jerry Lee Lewis, whose cousin Jimmy Swaggart became a well-known TV evangelist, went on to become a rock-and-roll icon. And, of course, in his brilliant, decades-long career, Johnny Cash recorded many more gospel and gospel-influenced songs.

In October 1960, Elvis began recording his first full-length gospel album, which would be titled *His Hand in Mine*. Released late that year, it stayed on *Billboard*'s Top LP chart for twenty weeks, reaching as high as number 13—a fitting tribute to both Elvis' popularity across stylistic lines and the sincerity with which he performed his beloved gospel music. *His Hand in Mine* included a good variety of favorite gospel songs previously recorded by the Golden Gate Quartet and other groups.

By this time, his popularity was such that it began to alter Elvis' life profoundly. Because of his recording popularity coupled with his status as a movie star, a huge stir erupted any time he went out in public. On one Easter Sunday, Elvis had to leave the Assembly of God Church in Memphis before the service was over, due to the uproar created by his presence. From that point on, attending a church service of any kind was out of the question. In fact, in a fan-magazine interview from this period, Elvis listed "not being able to attend church regularly" as one of his top ten dislikes. This may have been one important reason for his faithful attachment to gospel music: performing and gathering his friends together to sing the sacred songs he loved was, in some measure, Elvis' best chance to worship in the way he knew best. He also was fond of watching evangelists on television, with Rex Humbard's *Cathedral of Tomorrow* perhaps his most consistent favorite. Indeed, at a much later stage in Elvis' life, Humbard and his wife, Maude Aimee, would take part in perhaps the most profound spiritual experience Elvis ever knew.

Rex was Elvis' favorite preacher. Even if he was in the middle of a rehearsal, Elvis would always stop when Rex spoke on

Sunday mornings. Others who were close to Elvis at the time remembered that with the combination of preaching from television and the words and images of the gospel music he sang, Elvis managed to achieve what he thought was his closest possible approach to a "normal" devotional life. It was also probably no accident that *Cathedral of Tomorrow* featured one of the best quartets in the country, the Cathedrals.

"I don't think he understood at the time that he *was having a religious experience. But he definitely was, at the time he was singing those gospel songs."*

—Donnie Sumner

Another important aspect of his faith is demonstrated by Elvis' habitual—some would say reckless—generosity. Stories of Elvis purchasing and giving away gifts to relative strangers are well known. But those close to him also frequently benefited from his giving spirit. Elvis would often go out of his way to meet a personal need of someone in his entourage, be it financial, medical, or even spiritual.

Growing up in a Pentecostal church, Elvis saw God work powerfully. This aspect of his upbringing, not surprisingly, was often connected in Elvis' mind with his mother. I recall a conversation where Elvis asked probing questions about theology, including the nature and work of the Holy Spirit in the lives of believers. Elvis expressed a sense of unworthiness to be the recipient of his mother's vibrant faith heritage. "Mama had something real good," he said, "and I want what my mama had."

He frequently read the Bible and often prayed with those of us around him, both before going onstage and at other times. One evening he found out that a member of the Sweet Inspirations had been diagnosed with cancer. Elvis noticed, following a performance, that the women were upset, and asked why. When he found out, he immediately requested they go to the dressing-room area, where he asked them all to join him in prayer.

He prayed and he touched Sylvia's stomach, and he asked God to remove whatever it was, just take it away. And the next morning when Sylvia reported to Sunrise Hospital there in Vegas and they did the tests, it was gone. Whatever it was, whether it was a misdiagnosis, or whether God healed Sylvia through Elvis' faith and our faith, I don't know.

Now, please don't get the wrong idea: We didn't see Elvis as a miracle worker. Nobody reported Sylvia's healing to the press, and Elvis would have been the last person on earth who would have wanted to bring attention to such an incident. The fact is, such goings-on were just part of the culture during our time to-gether; it was the way life went. Though each of us had our own individual beliefs and faith, I don't think any of us regarded our-selves as super-spiritual, and we certainly didn't go around quot-ing scripture at each other. But we did share a common language and a common heritage: the same heritage that gave rise to gos-pel music. And that heritage was nowhere stronger and more important than in the mind and heart of the man who brought us all together to make music: Elvis Presley.

Chapter Three

RETURN TO THE STAGE

In the summer of 1968, thirteen months after his marriage to Priscilla Beaulieu and four months after the birth of their daughter, Lisa Marie, Elvis began preparation for his return to live performances. His first step was the taping of a television special, *Elvis*, at NBC Studios in Burbank, California. The show was a huge success with the audience and critics, which encouraged Elvis that the public was eager to see him in actual performance settings, rather than just on the big screen. A watershed event in Elvis' career among those who are fans, the show is usually just referred to as "the '68 Special."

One of the most notable segments of the special was a dramatic song written especially for the show by Earl Brown, "If I Can Dream." Elvis delivers perhaps the most stirring and heartfelt performance of the entire special, singing words speaking of justice and dignity for all mankind. No doubt, the recent assassinations of Bobby Kennedy and Martin Luther King, Jr.—the latter in Elvis' hometown, no less—gave the song's message much of its urgency. The simple yet powerful production of "If

I Can Dream" displays Elvis at his best: clad in white, standing on a darkened stage with a red neon "Elvis" backdrop, singing his heart out for the camera. For me, this segment of the show is so powerful because Elvis sings this song like a gospel singer; he seems completely carried away by the message, almost like someone in a trance. When he sings of "a better land / where all my brothers walk hand in hand," he seems to be transported there, in his imagination. No gospel performer ever had a more convicting message about a better place or a different way of living than Elvis does in "If I Can Dream." His voice wavers dangerously on the edge of roughness but never goes over. Instead, the overall impression is of a singer bringing every ounce of conviction and emotion he possesses to the song, reaching beyond the studio to connect powerfully with listeners' emotions. This, though not strictly a gospel song, speaks of Elvis' underlying sense of social fairness and his appreciation of the struggles faced by the disadvantaged—a group to which he originally belonged. As I listened and watched Elvis sing "If I Can Dream," I was mesmerized; the utter belief and meaning is so real in his face, his body, and his voice, I almost felt it grabbing hold of me each time I watched it.

Also included in *Elvis* is a lively production number comprised of a medley of songs starting with the hymn "Where Could I Go But to the Lord?," continuing with Lieber and Stoller's "I'm Saved," and ending with "Up Above My Head." Elvis is backed by the Blossoms, an African American female vocal group who would pave the way for his long affiliation with the Sweet Inspirations the following year.

Elvis' return to live performance was also fueled in part by his 1967 Grammy—the first in his career—for his sacred album,

How Great Thou Art. Recorded at RCA Studio B in Nashville during the early summer of 1966, the recording of this album gave me my first chance, as a member of The Imperials, a group recently formed by Jake Hess, to actually work with Elvis and his organization.

Accounts vary as to when Elvis first heard the title song, "How Great Thou Art," one of the all-time great gospel standards that came to be heavily identified with Elvis in later years. According to one version, Elvis' army buddy and fellow performer, Charlie Hodge, played a cut of the song for Elvis recorded by the Sons of the Pioneers—he may have also been familiar with the Statesmen's recording of the hymn. However, Ray Walker of the Jordanaires recalls talking with Elvis about the song at one of the sessions in Nashville, then going to his car for a hymnbook. Ray says that he and the Jordanaires sat with Elvis for over three hours going over the song and the harmonies. Both accounts may have some truth: Elvis may well have known the song, but sat with Ray and the Jordanaires to work out the exact arrangement he wanted to use for the recording session.

Myrna Smith of the Sweet Inspirations explains, *"Almost every time he sang that song, you could feel the spirit in him, because that was his actual praise to God."*

For the recording of the album, Elvis and Felton Jarvis, his producer, decided a choral sound would be appropriate for the musical background. Rather than bringing in an actual choir, though, they opted to stack the voices to sound like a choir, layering vocal-accompaniment tracks by the Jordanaires, Jake Hess and The Imperials, and a couple of strong female voices. The result was just the sound Elvis and Felton were looking for.

The song "How Great Thou Art" became a favorite of Elvis', a dynamic staple of his stage shows in later years. It seemed to all of us who worked with him that something special happened when Elvis sang this song; he really believed every word in it. In some particular way, "How Great Thou Art" displayed the soul of Elvis, a part of himself he was eager to share.

Despite the eventual critical and commercial success of *How Great Thou Art*, RCA label executives were not uniformly enthusiastic, at first, about the album's prospects, preferring instead that their star give the public more songs like "Heartbreak Hotel" and the other rock-and-roll hits that propelled his initial success. Elvis held firm, however, and the value of his persistence was validated abundantly when the album stayed on *Billboard*'s Top LPs chart for twenty-nine weeks. Sales exceeded one million dollars, and the Recording Industry Association of America certified a Gold Record for *How Great Thou Art* in February 1968.

Gordon Stoker recalls Elvis' determination: "RCA didn't want him to do gospel stuff. . . . He kept telling us we were going to do a gospel album, and so we finally got to do one, and it was a huge success."

Those of us close to Elvis have since noted that, in many ways, he was taking a tremendous career risk in his dogged determination to record gospel music. Nowadays, when we talk about an artist who does something like that—Bruce Springsteen, for example, doing a folk album—we're apt to comment about how gutsy an artist has to be to do material so far outside what he or she has previously been known for. We think that artist is doing something edgy and bold, staking out new territory in an effort to continue developing artistically and to expand his or her fan base. The fact is, that's exactly what Elvis was doing in his gospel work. Oh, sure, most artists will at some point do a Christmas album, especially if they're coming down to the end of a contract period and need something quick to fulfill their quota of material for the label. Some artists have even been known to put out an isolated hymn collection now and then. But recording gospel music was something Elvis Presley was determined to do, a calculated decision he pursued against the flow of pressure being brought to bear by label executives. One could easily wonder (and, no doubt, the RCA leadership did): What would the young generation think of "Elvis the Pelvis" performing sacred music? Would he ever be able to sell another rock-and-roll record? In retrospect, of course, all these fears proved groundless. As with all great artists who possess an unshakable vision of the sources of their inspiration, Elvis followed his heart, and *How Great Thou Art* confirmed the correctness of his judgment.

At the end of the summer of 1969, Elvis was scheduled to open a one-month engagement at Las Vegas' spectacular new International Hotel. The only performer booked there prior to Elvis was Barbra Streisand, and some have said the Colonel was content to let someone else work out the technical and logistic kinks of this untested performance space, so it didn't bother him that his boy wasn't first.

As Elvis began the process of planning whom he would invite to perform with him for this historic event, naturally his first choice for the group to provide his vocal backup was his favorite standby, the Jordanaires, who had been with him for over a decade. However, at this time, the quartet had so many recording sessions booked they didn't feel they could accept the offer. Elvis then remembered us, The Imperials, the singers who also worked with him on *How Great Thou Art*. He liked our sound and enjoyed our time together in the studio. Furthermore, he had been listening to our newer albums, on which we were demonstrating many of the new trends in Christian music beginning to gather popularity with listeners. Whatever went into the decision, the bottom line was Elvis liked our work, so he extended to us the chance of a lifetime—and we took it. On July 31, 1969, we stood on the stage as the curtain rose on Elvis Presley's first appearance before a non-studio audience in seven years. It seemed the whole world had been waiting for this moment.

As I've mentioned, a factor which may have been in The Imperials' favor is that during this period, we were a part of the newly emerging contemporary Christian music scene. While our roots were deep in traditional Southern and African American gospel, The Imperials were experimenting with different vocal arrangements, more contemporary instrumental backing, and a new approach to the material being written at that time. Elvis, whose championing of gospel music was starting to swing the attention of the pop music world toward sacred themes, apparently appreciated what we were trying to accomplish.

A lot of hard work, promotion, and hype went into transforming the International Hotel into "Elvis World." Anyone who knows anything about Elvis' life and work knows the show was a magnificent success. We played to a sold-out house, night after night; some audience members came to every show of the entire run. One of the greatest scenes, indicative of how important this engagement was to Elvis and the Colonel, came on the first night, at the close of the show. Elvis knew the performance had gone well, that the audience loved him, that everything about the evening had been magical. Backstage, after the curtain went down, the Colonel shoved his way through the crowd of us congratulating Elvis. The older man and his star looked at each other for a few seconds, then embraced each other. After a few back slaps, the Colonel excused himself and left, but not before some of us noticed that there were tears on his face. It was an impressive moment that communicated volumes.

We also soon discovered that performing for two audiences per night—starting at eight o'clock and midnight—was only one part of our job description.

"We did two shows a night for five weeks," Elvis once recalled in an interview. "Lots of times, we'd go upstairs and sing until daylight—gospel songs." Indeed, most nights, at some point, Elvis would ask us if we were coming to his suite after the midnight show. Naturally, we usually tried to make it a point to be there. On most occasions, there were a lot of people in the suite—by invitation only, of course. The Sweet Inspirations (the Sweets, for short) were usually there, all of The Imperials, and often several members of the TCB Band. The mix varied from night to night, but if we knew he wanted us up there—probably because he wanted to sing—we would do our best to show up. This held true for the length of The Imperials' engagement with Elvis, and it was the same with the Stamps, who replaced us as his backup singers a few years later. This was perhaps the most amazing experience of my life in show business; I have so many wonderful memories of those days and nights.

For many entertainers, leaving the stage means the end of singing for the day. But in Elvis' case, the end of the show was more like someone leaving work. Though Elvis was giving total concentration to and took great pride in his work onstage, he viewed the times up in his suite, singing or whatever else we might be doing, as "his" time. Some people play golf to unwind; some people jog or paint or read. For Elvis, the best way to unwind after a show was to sing gospel songs. Certainly he was energized by the enthusiasm of his audiences, but he was also driven by his innate love of gospel music. One of his favorite songs during these informal after-hours sessions was the spiritual "I, John, He Saw a Mighty Number." I don't suppose any of us who were there in those days could calculate how many times we gathered around a piano or someone with a guitar to sing this song with Elvis.

In fact, sometimes he would spring the song on us. Walking backstage before a performance, for example, he might wheel around to us and sing the first line: "I, John, he saw a mighty number . . ." The response he expected and received was the next phrase: "Way up in the middle of the air . . ." The words and cadences of gospel music were like some sort of secret code he shared with those of us who were close to him.

More than once, the invitees constituted a virtual Who's Who of Hollywood: Marty Allen, Lucille Ball, Redd Foxx, the Carpenters, Vikki Carr, and others. Sometimes it was a bit overwhelming to realize all these amazing, talented, and famous people were there to see the guy we were working for, the guy who made it a special point to invite all of us into his world.

It seemed as though Elvis took pleasure in "showing us off" to his visitors and guests, almost like a proud parent goading a child into playing a piano piece for relatives. It was important to him, somehow, that we showcase our music—gospel music—for the other people in the suite. Was he just showing that we were good singers, or was there a message he was trying to get across?

Ed Enoch of the Stamps remembers, "Every night when we finished, no matter what the time, we went upstairs and we sang to his friends."

I remember a very special occasion involving "Mama" Cass Elliot, when all of The Imperials were present. Her resonant voice captured millions in her recordings with the Mamas and the Papas as well as in her solo work. One night, as we were gathered around the piano singing, she said, "I'd like to sing 'Amazing Grace.' Would you guys back me up?"

Well, when one of the greatest recording artists in pop music history asks you if you'll sing backup for her, what else can you do? A couple of seconds later, I slid onto the piano bench and we began singing backup as Mama Cass sang a moving rendition of one of the best-loved hymns of all time.

It may have had something to do with the feeling a soloist gets when he or she is singing with a well-rehearsed group providing harmonic support. It's like leaning against a wall of sound, and it's an incredibly comforting sensation for a performer to feel. You don't get the sense of being all alone onstage; instead, the backup sort of wraps around you and gives you the confidence to really lose yourself in the music, to forget about yourself and focus on the act of communicating the message of the song to the audience. I think Mama Cass wanted to feel a little bit of what Elvis knew so well and experienced onstage each night.

At the end of "Amazing Grace," Mama Cass was visibly affected. She started hugging everyone, and the meaning of the song took on a life of its own in the room—even among those who had just been listening. I remember Elvis beaming like a proud daddy.

Another gospel song that held a special place in Elvis' attention was "Sweet, Sweet Spirit," written by Doris Akers. The Imperials recorded an a cappella version in the late 1960s, just before beginning our Las Vegas engagement with Elvis. He knew our album and was especially affected by this particular song. And when Elvis got a special feeling from a song, it often translated into knowing it would affect others, especially his fans.

I remember one occasion where he actually herded us into the large shower of his luxurious suite just so he could hear us sing "Sweet, Sweet Spirit" with the extremely live acoustics of the shower as a backdrop. Some of us sing in the shower, but not many of us could claim to have had a whole quartet sing there. I also remember that sometimes before a show, if we were ready with a few minutes to spare, he would take us all into the nearest men's room so he could hear the harmonies bounce off all the porcelain and tile. It amplified the sound in a weird way, but it was also nice.

Quite often, at a moment he would choose during the gatherings in his suite after the shows, Elvis would ask everyone to listen to us sing "Sweet, Sweet Spirit" a cappella. Once in a while, he actually had to stand up on the piano bench and wave his arms to quiet the group to a level he considered appropriate to the meaning of the song. Sometimes Elvis would request that those present bow their heads as they listened. In fact, it was sometimes amusing to observe the non-churchgoing folks in the group as they looked from side to side, probably a bit uncomfortable with this bit of "religious" behavior. I recall one occasion when, at Elvis' request, the guests in the suite were holding hands with their eyes closed and somebody looked up. Elvis said, "Put your head down." The guest complied, and we went on to sing the song Elvis requested. Gospel music was important enough to Elvis that he didn't mind insisting on a certain amount of reverence and decorum, even from people to whom the music was unfamiliar.

Most often, when we finally started singing the song, you could hear a pin drop. As we sang the opening words, "There's a sweet, sweet spirit in this place," I was often struck with the powerful sense that in these moments we were all equal: stars, musicians, crew members, what have you, and that we were somehow being brought together by the words of the song. "Sweet, Sweet Spirit" always garnered a quiet, positive, even worshipful reaction from the folks in the gathering, and Elvis usually seemed particularly moved by it. Time and again, as The Imperials finished this song, people would tell us they'd never heard anything like it. I don't want to detract at all from the power of the words and music themselves, but I remember with quiet pride the reaction we consistently received from our hearers. After J. D. Sumner and the Stamps began working with him as his Vegas backup group, Elvis sometimes made it a point to ask them to sing the song during live shows. He would introduce the song by saying something like:

"Ladies and gentlemen, if you would, I would like to ask the Stamps if they would sing a song that they do by themselves. It's a beautiful song called 'Sweet, Sweet Spirit.' And I don't sing in this; just listen to them, please." Then he would turn his back to the audience, facing the Stamps as they sang.

Looking back, it impresses many of us that by this simple gesture, Elvis was introducing a positive faith message to thousands upon thousands of fans and concertgoers, in Las Vegas and elsewhere, who probably never would have expected such an occurrence at one of "the King's" performances. Of course, neither I nor anyone else can presume that Elvis was consciously "evangelizing"; nothing more may have been involved than his simple love of this beautiful song. Still, for me the question is out there. I can't help believing that, for whatever reason, he loved the feeling he got when beautiful words combined with voices singing in close harmony.

The last line of "Sweet, Sweet Spirit" goes like this: "Without a doubt we'll know / that we have been revived / when we shall leave this place." I think Elvis was being revived when he heard us sing this song. And I think he wanted other people to feel it, too.

Chapter Four

ONSTAGE AND IN THE STUDIO WITH ELVIS

I magine yourself standing in a cavernous hall, dark except for piercing white strobe lights darting everywhere. The crowd knows the performer they have come to see is standing in the wings, waiting for his cue to come onstage. Their excitement comes at you like a tidal wave of pure adrenaline. A low, bass rumble pours from the huge speaker system: the opening notes of the *2001: A Space Odyssey* theme. Soon the three clear, cold notes of the opening trumpet call are answered by a crash of cymbals, then cascading strings and tympani as the music builds to an irresistible crescendo. The crowd responds and so do you; your pulse is hammering, even though you've experienced this opening almost every night for weeks. The drummer kicks in, pulling in the rest of the onstage ensemble, and a blinding white spot hits Elvis striding into view as he flashes that trademark smile at his public. He grabs a microphone and everyone onstage picks up the cue. In seconds, you are in the middle of a humming, throbbing entertainment machine.

Performing with Elvis in front of the wildly enthusiastic fans he attracted was an invigorating, utterly unforgettable experience. Any performer relishes the raw energy sensed when standing in front of a crowd having a great time, but Elvis was one of the most amazing entertainers in history. Like few others before or since, the magnetism of his personality emanated from the stage to the most distant seat in the house. He connected with his audiences as few ever have.

"Elvis Presley was a happening, and what he had going will never be again."

—*Joe Guercio*

One of the dominant public images of Elvis is as he was during the height of the Vegas years: often dressed in a white jumpsuit, turning a dramatic profile to the audience as he propels himself—and the rest of the singers and musicians—relentlessly through his repertoire. The main reason this image is so entrenched in the public imagination is that, night after night, Elvis delivered what his audiences loved.

For me, the road to Las Vegas began with a phone call in early July 1969. The Imperials were busy at that time: performing at gospel music shows, at "Jesus music" festivals, in concerts, at colleges, and on our own tours. We had a bus, we had bookings, we had albums out, and we were doing some backup work in the studio for other musicians—including, as I've mentioned, working with Elvis on *How Great Thou Art*. We had several guest appearances on network television shows: *The Joey Bishop Show*, *The Mike Douglas Show*, *The Tonight Show* with Johnny Carson. We were the only gospel group doing that sort of thing at the time; we sang backup for acts like Carol Channing and Pat Boone. That year, we won the Gospel Music Association's Dove Award for Best Male Group. Things were going well for us.

When the phone rang at our Music Row office in Nashville on that day in July, I answered, and heard the voice of Tom Diskin, Colonel Parker's right-hand man. He wanted to know if The Imperials were available for an engagement that would last the rest of July, August, and possibly part of September.

At first, I guess I was a little confused. "What kind of engagement would this be?" I asked. "I mean, yes, we've got bookings all during that time, but—"

"Well, Elvis Presley is opening at the new International Hotel in Las Vegas, and he'd like The Imperials to be his male backup group for the engagement."

I don't remember whether I was sitting down, but I should have been. I felt like jumping through the phone, or doing handsprings, or whatever else you can imagine. "Well, my goodness, I . . . of course, I'll have to talk to the rest of the guys to see what they think, and then I'll have to see if we can postpone our other bookings. . . ." I made a few such comments, doing my best to keep my voice normal, but all the while my mind was spinning like a runaway merry-go-round. *Elvis Presley! Two months at the International Hotel in Las Vegas! He wants us to back him!*

"Can you tell me any more about it?" I asked, stalling until I could get my thoughts reined in again.

"No, you fellas just talk it over and let me know if you can take the job. If you can, then we'll negotiate the money part, and all that."

I hung up, still trying to decide if I had just dreamed the whole thing. I decided I hadn't, and got together with the other guys: Jim Murray, Armond Morales, Terry Blackwood, and Roger Wiles. We had no idea how to price ourselves for the job; this was brand-new territory, not just for us, but for anybody, as far as I knew.

In fact, we spent a good deal of time discussing the implications of being gospel singers and going to Las Vegas—a locale not usually noted for gospel music. After all, we had built our success and our following in the world of gospel music and the mostly religious fans it attracted; how would our public feel about The Imperials appearing in a place like Las Vegas?

Still, this was an unprecedented, one-of-a-kind, once-in-a-lifetime opportunity—Elvis' first live concert for over ten years—and we really wanted to do it, as you can imagine. We wanted to do it enough that we figured out a way to smooth things over with our fans if anyone seemed offended by our presence in Las Vegas. In fact, we wanted to do it so badly we probably made a less advantageous deal for ourselves than we could have if we'd had cooler heads. We didn't want to oversell or undersell ourselves, so we came up with a price of $1,000 per week per musician, plus travel and other expenses. Tom Diskin told us we'd be paid the same during the rehearsal period as during the show's run, and this seemed like the way we should go.

Nowadays, of course, I know that such deals often include things like clothing allowances, per diem expense accounts, and other little things that have become pretty standard in the business. But, as I've said, this was brand-new territory. We called Tom back, made our offer, and pretty soon we had five airline tickets to Las Vegas. We didn't know if this was anything other than a thirty-day gig in Vegas, but we were backing Elvis Presley on his return to the live stage! We could hardly believe it was happening.

At that time, the International Hotel was the newest, biggest place in Vegas. There was no Mirage, no Bellagio, no MGM Grand, no Venetian. The show room seated 2,000, more than any other place in town. We got there and soon realized Elvis had been there for a couple of weeks already, rehearsing the TCB Band—the guitar, bass, drum, and keyboard combo that formed the heartbeat of the show. When we saw him the first time, Elvis was wearing wrist and ankle weights. He was in possibly the best physical shape of his life: about 175 pounds, tanned, and with the attitude of a champion racehorse about to go into the gate. It was impressive just being around him. He, of course, as was his usual way, did all he could to make everyone feel welcome. He made sure we were all introduced around to the other musicians, cracked jokes, told stories, and generally tried to promote a re-laxed, enjoyable atmosphere conducive to the type of intensive rehearsal we'd be doing in order to get the show ready.

While Elvis worked with the TCB Band, we went to another room and began working with the female backup singers, the Sweet Inspirations. We'd heard of them, of course. They re-corded on the Atlantic label and did tons of backup work, as well as having their own albums. They'd backed people like Aretha Franklin and Wilson Pickett, and collaborated with the likes of Carole King, Burt Bacharach, and Hal David. The Sweets were Myrna Smith, Sylvia Shemwell, Estelle Brown, and Cissy Hous-ton (you might have heard of her daughter, Whitney, just a little kid at this time). The Sweets got the gig as Elvis' female backups when the group he'd worked with on his 1968 TV special, the Blossoms, had a conflicting booking they couldn't rearrange.

The Sweets had an edgy soul sound, with Sylvia Shemwell at the core of that sound. Cissy was the "front" singer for the group. All of them had gospel music backgrounds, as I'll discuss more later. They came in with their entourage, including Cissy's husband, "Big John" Houston. We all got introduced and acquainted, and then Felton Jarvis, Elvis' producer, started working with us on the vocal arrangements. Before leaving Nashville, we'd received a list of about fifty songs we needed to learn, and with Felton's help we worked through each song, figuring out when to "ooh" and when to "ahh," when it would be just the Sweets or just The Imperials, and when it would be both. About three days into rehearsing—woodshedding—the arrangements, we joined Elvis and the TCB Band to start putting everything together.

It was magical. Of course, we had no idea we were making music and entertainment history—we were just having a great time! As you may know, in Las Vegas you never know what time it is. That was true during our rehearsals, as well; we had no idea if it was day or night, if we'd been going three hours or six—and we really didn't care. Everything was clicking, the band was unbelievably tight, our vocals were right on pitch and on cue, and we sensed, I think, we were melding together into something very, very special.

We went over and over the songs, preparing more material than we would ever use for a typical ninety-minute show. We were more than willing to put in the time required, however, honing the harmonies and transitions until the performing group had the organic cohesiveness Elvis required. Even though he was largely self-taught as a musician, we were continually impressed by the clarity and single-mindedness with which he pursued the exact sound he had in his mind. He knew exactly what he wanted, and we wanted more than anything to give it to him. Because of his lack of training, however, his main method of transferring his ideas to us was by demonstration, either singing the parts as he wanted to hear them or plunking them out on the piano as we followed along. The method was unsophisticated but effective. Furthermore, we all had such confidence in Elvis as a performer that we knew if we could give him what he was looking for, the show would be successful.

The fact was, Elvis was driven to do everything he could to make this show successful. As we've come to understand, it was pivotal to his return to industry prominence—and it was also an epoch-making event in Las Vegas. We rehearsed and perfected more material than we would need, simply because Elvis wanted us to. If someone were to call out a song or if Elvis decided, on the spur of the moment, to change up the order of the show or to substitute a number, he wanted us to be prepared to follow him seamlessly. If he threw in a karate move as part of his stage movement, he wanted the band ready to underline the action in just the right way. And that's how it went.

One of the reasons the instrumental and vocal backup group for the International show evolved as it did was because of the way Elvis' musical imagination and artistic conception continued to evolve. By the early 1970s, he had moved far beyond the young rock-and-roller who unleashed "Hound Dog" and "Heartbreak Hotel" on an unsuspecting world. Naturally, those early hits were huge crowd-pleasers and would continue to be an important part of the show, but Elvis' vision grew to include bigger, more expansive numbers that were almost operatic in their drama and musical sweep. To do songs like

"American Trilogy" and "Bridge Over Troubled Water" the way he envisioned, he needed the range of an orchestra behind him. To reach the intensity required for spiritual numbers like "How Great Thou Art," he wanted to have solid backup vocals wrapped around him. The Sweets gave him the black influence he needed for soul- or gospel-flavored tunes like "Polk Salad Annie" or the gospel standard "Amen." And, of course, when it was time for some good old-fashioned rock and roll, there was no tighter musical group than the TCB Band, especially with Ronnie Tutt on drums, who had the uncanny ability to anticipate what Elvis might do and provide the perfect accent. In other words, Elvis needed musicians who were also performers with wide versatility, able to accommodate everything from a sweeping orchestral interlude to hand-clapping gospel to straight-ahead rock and roll. And by the time the show opened at the end of July, that was exactly what he had.

A couple of days before the show opened, we moved into the show room at the International where we would play to sold-out houses for fifty-eight consecutive shows. The atmosphere in the hotel was like a carnival, thanks to the tireless promotional efforts of Colonel Parker. Add a forty-piece orchestra to the mix, and the result was outrageous—a musical and entertainment extravaganza that would break all records.

Often, just before the show began as we gathered in the wings, Elvis would turn to someone standing nearby. "Lead us in a prayer for the show," he would say. A quick but sincere prayer would follow as, with eyes closed and heads bowed, we would join together to ask for the ability to accomplish successfully what we had prepared to do.

Once we were all onstage and the show was in progress, our

only thought was to focus on the material and the moment. Personal chemistry was very important to Elvis, and he liked to look over during a number and see that his performers were having a good time and giving one hundred percent to the audience.

He expected no less of himself. On an occasion when Elvis was having a vocal problem due to a cold, Bill Baize remembers Elvis slipping away from Red and Sonny at the last second. It was time for the curtain to go up and they were frantically searching for him everywhere, but Elvis was nowhere to be found. Finally, they opened the door of the men's room and there he was, kneeling down, praying, and asking God to help him to be able to touch his fans with the music on that particular night.

Elvis was clearly born for the concert stage. He loved to perform, but it's important to remember that his greatest inspiration didn't originate from the footlights out—he really didn't care whether the crowd numbered 1,000 or 20,000. His truest inspiration came onstage with his musicians and his singers; this was his domain. We all knew that, and so we all tried to be our best at all times. When he looked over at us, we had to be smiling, we had to be focused, and it was almost like we were his cheerleaders. And if he saw us reacting that way, it ratcheted his performance up a notch.

The way Elvis selected his material was that he usually programmed the early hits everybody wanted to hear—"Hound Dog," "Heartbreak Hotel," "Blue Suede Shoes," "Teddy Bear," and others like that—in a medley format. We'd spin through these rather quickly, and the crowds loved them, of course. But when it came time to do songs Elvis believed held a special message—"In the Ghetto," "Walk a Mile in My Shoes," or "Don't Cry, Daddy," for example—he would often stop and give some sort of spoken intro to the song, as if to make sure the audience received the message he was trying to send. I'm not sure Elvis ever realized it, but the words he used to introduce "Walk a Mile in My Shoes" were actually penned by Hank Williams:

You never stood in that man's shoes, or saw things through his eyes,
Or stood and watched with helpless hands while the heart inside you dies.
So help your brother along the way, no matter where he starts.
For the same God that made you, made him too: these men with broken
hearts.

Though he shared an amazing connection with his audiences, Elvis also maintained a sort of surprised humility about his fame and fortune. He never forgot where he came from. This was illustrated powerfully at a concert near the campus of Notre Dame University. Apparently, a large group of female students purchased seats stretching completely across the middle of the auditorium. They made preparations, and at the moment during the show they judged best, they all stood, holding up a huge banner that said, ELVIS, YOU'RE THE KING. Tony Brown remembers what happened next:

And Elvis just stopped and pointed at them. "No. Jesus Christ is the King," he said. And they just sat down immediately, totally embarrassed. And we went on to the next song. But it sent chills up my spine. He wasn't mad at them, but he made a point. And it was amazing that the reviewer never mentioned it, or anything. But I will never forget it; it was a big moment for me.

In 1972, Elvis was preparing to record another gospel album, *He Touched Me.* He had it in his mind he wanted a certain bass singer for the backup group, and even though the man had ceased active performance work years before, Elvis was determined to find him.

Elvis was always fascinated by bass singers, by the resonance of their low notes. He once told Ray Walker of the Jordanaires, "the Lord messed up when He didn't make me a bass singer."

The Harmonizing Four, an African American gospel group, recorded a song called "Let's Go to that Land," which featured a catchy bass lead in the chorus. Elvis loved this song and hoped to find and hire the singer who recorded the original version. The word went out, and a search was made throughout the South (the group was originally from Georgia), to no avail. Finally, though, the man was located in South Carolina. Unfortunately, he hadn't sung in years and was no longer in good health. For these reasons, he was unable to join us, even for a few shows, so Elvis could show off his bass singing.

Although Elvis poured himself into every song he recorded, he was especially fond of his gospel recording sessions. Without the pressure of producing radio hits, he had the freedom to approach these albums as he pleased.

A standard recording session lasts three hours, at whatever rate per hour is stipulated by the rate schedule the studio and musicians use to set their fees. For example, by the late 1960s, the Jordanaires were scheduling three to four sessions per day, which was why they felt they couldn't take the job with Elvis in Las Vegas. When we worked on the sessions that included some of the gospel material for *He Touched Me*, The Imperials were booked at an hourly rate for twelve hours straight, from

6:00 P.M. until 6:00 A.M., every day for two weeks. We were told, "Just come on in to the studio, and when Elvis shows up, we'll record." Elvis finally arrived at about 11:00 P.M., and by 12:30 he was ready to listen to some songs as possibilities for recording.

Usually, several people would be pitching songs to Elvis, hoping he'd like one well enough to put it on the record. He'd listen, and if he was intrigued, he might sit down at the piano and start working out some of the chords and voicings. Meanwhile, the singers would be in another corner, "oohing" and "ahhing," figuring out where and when the backup lines should be placed. At the same time, the musicians were jotting down chord symbols, figuring out the tempos, and working on transitions. By the time Elvis decided he liked the song, we tried to be ready. But if Elvis opted not to do the song we just sort of hung loose, waiting to see if the next idea started to develop some creative momentum.

Sometimes people would have an acetate recording of a song: "Listen to this one, Elvis; see what you think." And a similar process would start. If Elvis was enjoying himself, strolling around the studio with a mike, we'd keep going. If he was getting bored or impatient, we'd stop. We might work for three or four hours, or we might go for twelve hours straight, all depending on whether Elvis heard the sound in his head he was looking for.

Elvis could be somewhat unfocused in the studio. He didn't behave exactly in accord with the images you may have seen on television or the movies: sitting on a stool in a booth with earphones, in front of a mike, doing take after take until it was perfect. Elvis tended to wander more, holding the mike in his hand—almost as if he were onstage in front of a crowd. This was his favored mode of operation, and as a result, many of his recordings lack the technical perfection some would have wanted.

What he lost in production technique, though, he made up in the conviction of his delivery, especially in his gospel recording sessions, which always started with one of Elvis' favorite settings: gathered with a quartet around the piano. Here, he tended to be more attentive than in other studio settings. This is not surprising given his love for the music.

"With Elvis, if it was a rhythm song, he had that mike in his hand, and he was going through all of his gyrations and his moves to the rhythm of the music. He could not be still on a rhythm song."

—*Terry Blackood*

Both in the recording studio and onstage, Elvis was fearless in terms of things he would try that he thought might enhance his performance. He might sing several steps higher than any of us thought his range should be, if he was going for a "big finish" on a song. Or he might reach deep in his bass register to add some extra punch to a chorus. For him, the only thing that mattered was getting the sound he wanted, from himself and from everyone else.

RCA was still pushing Elvis to do more pop records, but in the meantime they were shipping and selling thousands and thousands of his gospel recordings. Not surprisingly, *He Touched Me* was on *Billboard*'s Top LPs chart for ten weeks, and garnered Elvis his second Grammy, for Best Inspirational Performance. I can't help believing that somewhere in his mind, Elvis knew he was making his mother proud.

In 1971, The Imperials' time as Elvis' backup group came to a close. Not surprisingly, as he searched for our replacements he thought of the man he'd admired so much as a youth and who was still close to him, J. D. Sumner, and his quartet, the Stamps. J.D. had, of course, remained very connected to the gospel music world, most recently by means of his talent and booking organization, the Sumar Agency (a blending of the first syllables of his last name and the first name of his wife, Mary). The agency had been active since the late 1960s; in fact, The Imperials were clients. J.D. was tuned in to the industry and was eager to build the roster of groups under his representation. I had the opportunity, at J.D.'s invitation, to find prospects for the agency among the up-and-coming groups on the touring scene; I also acted as Sumar's goodwill ambassador at gospel music sings and gatherings. For all of these reasons, it seemed natural that when Elvis thought of someone to take the place The Imperials held, J. D. Sumner was foremost in his mind. He invited the Stamps to join his entourage, and they accepted.

Though the male backup singers changed, the electricity of Elvis' performance remained. He continued to play to sold-out houses. In fact, in 1971 he was awarded a special trophy belt-buckle by the City of Las Vegas in recognition of the record-breaking attendance at his shows.

The other thing that didn't change was Elvis' love of gospel music and the after-show singing sessions in his suite, sessions that sometimes lasted all night. And just because The Imperials weren't in Elvis' show any longer, that didn't bump us from the list of invitees for the all-night sings in his suite. Sherman Andrus, who joined The Imperials after our engagement with Elvis concluded, remembers:

We were working with Jimmy Dean in Las Vegas. And we'd have to wait until our last night with Jimmy Dean, because we knew if we went over to Elvis' suite, he would have us sing all night. We'd go there and we'd start whenever our second show was over, and we would go until about six or seven in the morning, just singing songs, hanging out, or whatever Elvis wanted—which included lots of gospel music.

Despite the fatigue we might have felt at the time, we sensed how important it was to Elvis that we be there for him and be able to provide him the opportunities to share with his guests and all of us his love for the music. As Ed Enoch of the Stamps said, "At that time it wasn't as enjoyable for me, because of being tired and wanting to take a break from it after singing so many hours. But if I had that opportunity, I would do it again. I'd sing just as long as I could stay up. I think right there was where I found the real Elvis Presley."

Elvis said of gospel music, "We grew up with it, from the time I can remember, like two years old. It more or less puts your mind at ease. It does mine." Those of us who were near Elvis during these years sensed how important the gospel music was to his state of mind. To us, he seemed most himself when he was in the midst of the musicians and others whom he considered his family, singing the music he first heard as a child—the music his mother gave him. This was where Elvis was able to find his center, even amid the razzle-dazzle of the Las Vegas showbiz routine. When Elvis sang gospel, he was at peace.

Chapter Five

Trials, Faith, and a Giving Heart

Though his most ardent fans thought he could do no wrong, Elvis was well aware of his shortcomings, and he grew increasingly uncomfortable with the adulation lavished upon him. Though it might seem surprising to some, observing not only his overwhelming success but also the talent and energy he brought to his performances, Elvis could seem almost insecure, at times, about everything that came his way.

"I think that Elvis thought that he'd wake up and find that it was all over with, that it was just a dream."

—*Ed Enoch*

Elvis wasn't backward about giving credit for his success to God. When it was pointed out to Elvis how blessed he was, he responded, "I know that. And I know that I couldn't have done it without God." He once told a magazine reporter, "I never expected to be anybody important. Maybe I'm not now. But whatever I am, whatever I will become, will be what God has chosen for me. I feel He's watching every move I make."

Even though Elvis was often confused about why God allowed him such success and acclaim, he never questioned that his gifts were from God. Perhaps that's why the song "He Touched Me" was particularly meaningful to him. When Elvis was taken with a song, he approached it like an obsession, and this was the case with "He Touched Me." J. D. Sumner once told of being on tour with Elvis when he secured the use of a stereo and proceeded to listen to "He Touched Me" perhaps as many as fifty times in a row.

The depth of this conviction may also explain why his performance of "How Great Thou Art" from his LP *Elvis: Recorded Live on Stage in Memphis* was awarded a Grammy for Best Inspirational Performance in 1974.

"The big people don't need me. It's the little people that need me."

—*Elvis Presley*

As a person who came up in hard circumstances, the biblical admonition to care for the poor and disenfranchised was close to Elvis' heart. During the 1960s and early 1970s, tensions between blacks and whites were at an all-time high. Elvis demonstrated his desire for racial reconciliation in the musicians he chose, and in the treatment they received. A shining example of his advocacy for causes he considered just came not long after Elvis' return to the concert stage, when he made his first appearance in Texas, in the Astrodome. According to Myrna Smith of the Sweet Inspirations, Elvis was told, "Well, you can leave the black girls home. You don't have to bring them." But Elvis wasn't going to do the Astrodome unless "his girls" could be with him. He demanded that we be given the same star treatment as everyone else: we'd ride in our convertible into the Astrodome where everybody could see us. That was his statement: "You don't like it, deal with it, or I'm not going to be there." We were so impressed with the stand he took on our behalf, and we thanked him for it.

Sherman Andrus joined The Imperials in 1972, after we finished our time with Elvis, but that didn't mean he wasn't considered a member of "the family." As one of the first African Americans to appear with a contemporary or Southern gospel group, he was sensitive to being thought of as conspicuous. "They took a chance, because there were no blacks in contemporary or Southern gospel music," he said. "I was the first one, and it made the headlines, and it was in *Billboard*, and all the newspapers in Tennessee." Andrus recalls, however, that upon his first meeting with Elvis—he was invited to the suite after a show, with the rest of The Imperials—he was made to feel absolutely at ease. Elvis even showed him a file of clippings about Andrus he had collected. He went on to give Sherman a TCB necklace, symbolic of being in the inner circle, and Andrus recalls how important it was at that moment to feel not only accepted but like one of the guys. "For a guy who didn't really know where he stood, this was very important to me. He acknowledged my presence and made me feel very much a part of what we were all doing. Right away, he treated me like he'd known me for years. He gave me one of those coveted TCB necklaces and I was just one of the guys. And I never forgot that." (TCB stands for Taking Care of Business, and Elvis gave all of us in his entourage, and some very close friends, these fourteen-karat gold necklaces to identify us and separate us from the others. They became very coveted and in demand. He also had some TLC [Tender Loving Care] neck-laces made for the ladies, which he gave out occasionally. There is no doubt the original necklaces are worth quite a bit now, as collectors' items. His band was also known as the TCB Band.)

I have always believed that this conviction about the worth of every human being, regardless of racial or other differences, is what animated and empowered Elvis' performance of "If I Can Dream" on his 1968 television special. The sincerity of his ex-pression and his delivery of that song are too unmistakable for me to think otherwise. Another type of scene that comes vividly to mind is of Elvis standing onstage, speaking from his heart to the audience as he introduced one of his "message" songs, such as "Walk a Mile in My Shoes." When he did that, it was more than the emotional lead-in to some song in a show; he was speak-ing about what he truly believed.

Elvis never forgot the pain of poverty. He was so thankful for what came his way, and he felt compelled to share it with others. His generosity may have also been somewhat motivated by the subconscious belief that his wealth was inexhaustible. His custom of giving away one-thousand-dollar checks to scores of Memphis charities at Christmas is well known, as is his penchant for pur-chasing cars for other people—sometimes for perfect strangers. In fact, he bought so many cars for other people, no accurate record exists. If television preaching was his sermon and gospel music was his praise, it follows that such acts of benevolence represented to Elvis his "tithe": the way he carried out what he viewed as his faith-based responsibility to give back a portion of what he received in a way that would benefit others.

I remember one amusing incident—well, kind of an embarrassing one really—that happened near the end of one of our runs with Elvis in Las Vegas. It was E's custom to give gifts to his fellow performers at the end of each run: these were beautiful, expensive gifts. At the end of this particular run, he selected some exquisite, custom-made wristwatches for the group. There were fewer than a hundred of them made, and they were self-winding, which was quite the thing at the time. They had *Elvis Presley* inscribed at the top of the bezel and five stars at the bottom—they were absolutely gorgeous.

The only trouble was, mine wouldn't run. I'd shake my wrist, twist it back and forth every which way, and still my watch wouldn't go. One night, before the show, I decided to tell Elvis about it. It sort of makes me blush, now, to think of the audacity of complaining to the person who'd given me such an expensive gift—literally looking the proverbial gift horse in the mouth—but that was what I decided to do.

So I went down the hall to E's dressing room, knocked on the door, told whoever was there that I needed to speak to Elvis. I'm looking over his shoulder as he's in the midst of getting dressed and made up for the show, and I say, "Elvis, this watch is beautiful and I love it and really appreciate it and all that, but it won't run."

Without missing a beat, Elvis said, "I just give 'em away; I don't fix 'em."

Oh, man, was I embarrassed. I went back to my dressing room

with my tail between my legs and I don't think I ever mentioned that watch again to anybody. I still have it, though—and it still doesn't run.

Some people may wonder whether Elvis' lavish giving was some sort of grandstanding act, a means to impress others. But those of us who had an opportunity to actually feel it and know the sincerity of it realized his giving spirit was truly a part of his nature. My family was the personal recipient of Elvis' generosity —one night in 1972 when, during a run with Jimmy Dean in Las Vegas, we received the jolting news that our home in Nashville had been broken into. We were invited up to Elvis' suite after the second show, and somewhere around three o'clock or three-thirty in the morning, as we were gathered around the piano singing, one of Elvis' entourage pulled me aside and said, "Your wife is on the phone and she's hysterical." I went to the phone and my wife, calling in tears from our motel room, informed me she just received notification from the authorities in Franklin, the Nashville suburb where we lived at the time.

Elvis' first reaction was to turn to Sonny West, one of his closest assistants. "Sonny, get the plane ready."

"What do you mean?" Sonny asked.

"Get the plane ready. We're going to Nashville."

Elvis was so riled up by the notion that someone had robbed our home that he was ready to load everybody up and fly to Nashville—right then and there. Gradually, though, he was per-suaded this might not be the most productive alternative, since he had a show to do that night. Still, he insisted on going to our hotel and doing what he could to help the situation. In a few minutes, there was a caravan of white limos rolling up in front of the hotel where I was staying with my wife and children. My wife met me at the door, still extremely upset, and by now my children were wide awake and crying. I'll never forget the scene.

I'll also never forget the look on my kids' faces when Elvis Presley stepped out of his limo and walked through the door to comfort my family. It was as though a superhero had arrived to save the day. He hugged my wife and told her not to worry; he assured her that everything was going to be okay. "I'll get to the bottom of this," he told her.

Soon the front room of our little suite looked like the command post for a police operation. Elvis was giving orders for Felton Jarvis, the show's producer, who also lived in Franklin, to call the sheriff there and get the precise facts on the situation. He was having the time of his life, I think; this was out of the ordinary, an adventure.

"The Imperials never met a kinder man, a more generous man, who cared about people, and he made us feel so welcome, every time we were with him."

—Terry Blackwood

In the meantime, Elvis noticed our children in the other room. He went in there and sat down on the bed in the middle of them, telling them not to worry about anything. "Look, this is no problem," he told them. "I'm really sorry this happened to you all, and I want you to know that if they took any of your things, like your bicycle or anything, I'll get you another one, and it'll be better than the one you had. I'll replace everything better than what you had. Don't you worry about it."

What parent wouldn't be grateful for anyone who would show such kindness, gentleness, and consideration to his children? But in my kids' eyes this wasn't just anyone: this was Elvis.

IN 1971, ELVIS WAS RECOGNIZED by the national Jaycees organization as one of the top ten outstanding young men in America. As was typical for him in serious, reflective moments, he used his acceptance speech as an opportunity to make reference to his faith:

> When I was a child, ladies and gentlemen, I was a dreamer. I read comic books and I was the hero of the comic book. I saw movies and I was the hero in the movie. So every dream that I ever dreamed has come true a hundred times. And these gentlemen over here, [points to other nine award recipients on the platform] you see these type people who care, that are dedicated. You realize that it's just possible that they might be building the kingdom of Heaven. It's not too far-fetched from reality. I'd like to say that I learned very early in life that without a song, the day would never end. Without a song, a man ain't got a friend. Without a song, the road would never bend—without a song. So I'll keep singing a song.

Elvis was a voracious reader, and he was extremely open minded— so much so, in fact, he would give serious consideration to anyone who approached him with what could be considered a path to spirituality. I sometimes wondered if, because of his worldwide celebrity status, Elvis somehow felt obligated to consider all the alternatives presented to him. Also, his natural humility and courtesy would likely have inhibited him from dismissing anyone's ideas out of hand.

In the latter years, the hectic pace and exhausting schedule of the tours and concerts began to take its toll not only on Elvis but on those around him. People would leave the entourage for other opportunities, and other people came in. It's possible the thought that should have been given to inviting previously unknown people into the very intimate, intensely interpersonal setting that existed in Elvis' organization was occasionally somewhat lacking.

As new people came in, they brought new ideas and agendas with them, and, of course, everyone wanted Elvis' ear. Numerology, astronomy, and non-traditional philosophical and religious ideas found their way to Elvis, despite the misgivings often felt—and sometimes voiced—by those closest to him.

Certainly, there were times when he seemed confused and even perplexed by questions that seemed to have no ready answers. But somehow, his roots and his mother's early training always called him back. I remember thinking that if we could "settle him down" by singing gospel music, he'd soon be himself again.

Without question, in his life of fame and riches, Elvis encountered many temptations. He succumbed to some of them—and who among us, having been placed in a similar situation, can say for certain we wouldn't do the same? But I believe that somewhere deep inside, those early beliefs stayed alive and active, propelling him forward even when he wasn't sure where he was headed. And the way those beliefs most often found expression in his daily life was in the singing and enjoyment of gospel music.

No doubt this impulse was what motivated him, during one of the singing sessions in his suite, to request that everyone stop what they were doing and form a circle, holding hands. When this was done, he announced, "I want The Imperials to sing a song, and I want everyone to close their eyes and listen." Then he asked us to sing "He Touched Me." This was a classic Elvis moment: taking advantage of his star status to share through a favorite song the sincerity of his belief, even with those who might have been a bit hesitant to receive such a gift. As I looked around the circle, I saw people from every walk of life: from the rich and famous to the average and unknown. But the one thing we had in common during that moment was our wish to be respectful of our host's request. He was offering up a bit of himself, revealing a side of his life that the adoring masses didn't have the opportunity to witness. He was putting into view, whether everyone there fully realized it or not, the gospel side of Elvis.

Chapter Six

ALL THE KING'S
MEN . . . AND WOMEN

Because his musical conception was so influenced by the quartet style, Elvis' career can almost be traced by tracking the backup singers he worked with at various times. From his earliest days, he loved the feeling of the "wall of sound" provided by voices singing in close harmony. You can hear it in songs as diverse as "Don't Be Cruel" and "He Touched Me." It's such a part of the "Elvis sound" that it sometimes gets taken for granted. But Elvis never took it for granted; having the right backup voices was as important to him as having the right songs to sing.

First, of course, were the Jordanaires. They were also the group that worked the longest with Elvis, though, of course, the actual roster changed from time to time. The original group—made up of Bill and Monty Matthews, Bob Hubbard, Culley Holt, and pianist Bob Money—formed in 1948, and by the time Elvis first worked with them in 1956, the Jordanaires were already some of the most successful recording musicians in the South, having worked with stars such as Eddy Arnold and Patsy Cline.

Gordon Stoker, who replaced Money on piano in 1951 and also sang tenor when needed, sang with Elvis in a January 1956 RCA session that included "I Got a Woman," "Heartbreak Hotel," and "Money Honey." Ben and Brock Speer, of the gospel greats the Speer Family, also sang on this session. Early the following summer, the group backed Elvis' sound-track recording for his second appearance on *The Milton Berle Show*. The Jordanaires would go on to record well over one hundred songs with Elvis; they were his backup group for more than fifteen years.

I'm sometimes asked if some sort of falling-out occurred, preventing the Jordanaires from working Elvis' Las Vegas opening in 1969. Nothing could be further from the truth. Elvis and the Jordanaires had a great relationship, and why not? They were fantastic for each other. The simple fact is that in 1969, no one knew for sure whether Elvis' Vegas opening signified anything more than a one-time gig. Since the Jordanaires at that time were booked for several sessions a day every day for months in advance, earning significant money and adding to their well-earned respect in the recording industry, they made a sound decision when they regretfully declined Tom Diskin's invitation to come to Las Vegas with Elvis.

For The Imperials, however, as I've mentioned, the opportunity, though not without its potential downsides, proved to be life-changing. Again, we had to rearrange, postpone, or cancel a number of previous engagements at concerts, Jesus music festivals, and other events in order to clear our calendars for the Vegas run, but it was worth it; we really wanted to be there.

I've already told a bit about what it was like to rehearse and perform with Elvis, but I'd like to explain how our time with Elvis came to an end. Much like the Jordanaires' situation, our

decision to leave the show came about due to business considerations, pure and simple. I've already said we were in a bit of a
quandary in figuring out how to price our services in response
to the phone call from Tom Diskin; we finally settled on a fee of
$1,000 per week per man, plus expenses. After we played Vegas
twice a year during 1969, 1970, and 1971, plus other concert
appearances and recording sessions, we thought it was time to
request an improved compensation arrangement. The Colonel,
ever one to drive a hard bargain on behalf of his boy, didn't see
things our way, and it soon became apparent we needed either to
resign ourselves to working for the same package or to find other
opportunities. We made a number of contacts, however, one of
whom was Jimmy Dean, who also had a very successful show
playing in Las Vegas, Tahoe, Reno, on the West Coast, and in
other locations. He also had a television show. We negotiated an
arrangement that allowed us to work for his stage shows and also
guaranteed us a spot on each episode of the television show—all
for a bit more money than we were making with Elvis. It seemed
like a prudent decision to make the change, and the idea of singing gospel music on a nationally syndicated television show was
very appealing. So, like the Jordanaires before us, we regretfully
came to the decision to end our time with Elvis. As I've mentioned, though, we parted on the very best of terms. We had
an open invitation to join him anytime, and would spend many
more hours in Elvis' suite after the show, singing until sunrise.

When Elvis learned of our decision to go with Jimmy Dean,
he asked for our recommendations for a group to replace us.
We told him there were really only two groups we could recom-
mend: J. D. Sumner and the Stamps, and the Oak Ridge Boys.
The trouble with the Oak Ridge Boys at that time, though, was

they were moving from gospel to country music; their style and musical direction might not be the best fit for Elvis' needs. So the logical choice for Elvis to make was to call J.D., which is exactly what he did.

Because of the deep and longstanding admiration Elvis held for J. D. Sumner and vice versa, it was hard to tell who was more pleased by the new arrangement with the Stamps. Elvis would introduce J.D. by announcing to the audience, "Ladies and gentlemen, here's a man that I've known since I was fourteen years old. He's the greatest bass singer in the world, and I never thought I'd get to share his stage. Thank you, J.D., for letting me share your stage."

No doubt, a portion of Elvis' appreciation of J.D. had to do with his abiding love of bass singers. He would do anything he could, in a show or in the private "sings" in his suite, to select songs featuring the low bass range. J.D. was billed as "the lowest bass singer in the world," and Elvis tried to capitalize on that any way he could.

Such was Elvis' confidence in J.D. and the Stamps that he soon offered them the chance to open the show. He also made an impromptu request for the Stamps to sing "Sweet, Sweet Spirit" during a performance. Elvis asked J.D. to take center stage on one occasion, when he had to leave the hall momentarily. J.D. rose to the occasion, not only keeping the crowd from becoming restive, but actually winning them over.

J. D. Sumner held a huge, lifelong place in Elvis' admiration. Maybe it was because J.D. took an interest in Elvis when he was a boy who couldn't afford a ticket to hear his beloved gospel music. Maybe it was because of J.D.'s powerful bass voice. Maybe it was because heroes, once they've staked a claim in our minds, never really leave us. Many of us considered Elvis' attitude toward J.D. very much one of hero worship.

Ed Enoch of the Stamps, recalling their unexpected performance: "It was at a concert, and he just called us out. Nobody knew about it; we didn't know we were going to do it at all. It really put us on the map, so to speak. . . . People knew who we were."

The Sweet Inspirations, as a group, were "on" more consistently than almost any performers I've ever known. It seemed these ladies just never had a bad night. In the late 1960s they got a Grammy nomination for their single, "Sweet Inspiration," and that song reportedly attracted Elvis' attention. When the Blossoms, who backed him on the '68 Special, were unable to come to Vegas in 1969 because of prior commitments, Elvis didn't hesitate; he signed the Sweets with no audition required.

The Sweets' roots were deep in gospel music; all of them grew up singing in church, either as soloists or in choirs. Cissy Houston was born Cissy Drinkard; she was a member of the Drinkard Singers, the first group to have a gospel album released on a major label (a live recording from the Newport Jazz Festival in 1959). I mentioned earlier that Cissy was the mother of superstar Whitney Houston; I should also say she was the aunt (though only seven years older) of Dionne Warwick, whose hits included "Do You Know the Way to San Jose?" and "Walk On By." In fact, Dionne and her sister Dee Dee were founding members of the group; Cissy took Dionne's place when Warwick's solo career began to take off. At the same time, Sylvia Shemwell replaced Doris Clay. In 1965, Dee Dee left and Myrna Smith joined. This was the group that recorded for Atlantic in 1967. Their self-titled hit, "Sweet Inspiration," would be recorded by artists as diverse as Barbra Streisand and Dusty Springfield.

The Sweets were successful in gospel, R & B, and pop music; they could do it all. In 1968, as Cissy Drinkard and the Sweet Inspirations, they recorded a gospel album, *Songs of Faith and Inspiration*. Though Cissy Houston left the group after the August 1969 Vegas run, the Sweets stayed with Elvis from that first live show until his death in 1977.

In 1973, after weathering the divorce from Priscilla, Elvis approached Donnie Sumner with a somewhat unusual proposition. He wanted a group that would always be available to come wherever he was, whenever he wanted it. He would pay the musicians an appropriate retainer, but he would expect them to come when he called—whenever he felt the need for someone to sing with. Actually, Elvis tried to get this group a gig with Tom Jones, who was reportedly looking for a male backup group. When the opportunity with Jones didn't come through, Elvis offered to put them on his payroll.

The group, dubbed Voice, could be seen as the culmination of Elvis' wishes and customs almost from the time his career began. During The Imperials' time with him in Vegas and on tour, we were expected to attend the after-hours singing sessions in Elvis' suite. The same was true for the Stamps. At this point in his career, as self-doubt and bouts with depression began to prey on Elvis' mind, he longed more than ever for the solace he found in gospel music. Voice was a means to assure himself of the constant availability of that solace.

The members of Voice were drawn from among the musicians Elvis knew and loved: Donnie Sumner, nephew of J. D. Sumner and former lead singer for the Stamps; Tony Brown, who played piano for several gospel groups, including the Stamps; Sherrill (later Shaun) Nielsen, formerly of The Imperials and the Statesmen; and Tim Batey, who had previously sung with both the Stamps and the Statesmen. They were all familiar to Elvis and to each other.

Maybe this is a good place to explain a bit about how interconnected the relationships were in the gospel music world. A photo in this book shows J. D. Sumner and the Stamps as they were in the mid-1960s. Pictured are Tony Brown, Donnie Sumner, Mylon LeFevre, Jim Hill, J.D., and Jimmy Blackwood. Tony and Donnie, of course, I've already mentioned in connection with the Stamps. Mylon LeFevre, born into the gospel family the Singing LeFevres, wrote the song "Without Him," which was not only included by Elvis on his *How Great Thou Art* album, but went on to be recorded by over a hundred other gospel artists, including the Gaithers, as well as becoming a worship favorite of churches across the nation. In later years, Mylon, with his group Broken Heart, would become known to a whole new generation of contemporary Christian music fans. Jimmy Blackwood was the son of James Blackwood, one of the original Blackwood Brothers who sang at Gladys Presley's funeral (and remember that J.D. was a member of the Blackwoods, also). Elvis, of course, knew all this; he knew the musicians, knew their pedigrees, knew who they performed with, probably owned every album on which they appeared, and knew precisely what he liked or didn't like about the way they sounded. After all, this is the guy who knew I was the piano player for the Harmoneers, which was not exactly a household name at the time.

Elvis realized the Stamps, because of their other commitments for performances and recording, couldn't always be available to him. The same was true for The Imperials and certainly the Jordanaires, who hadn't really performed with him consistently since his Vegas opening in 1969. But he still needed to sing gospel music—it was almost an addiction, it seemed.

So a typical schedule for Voice might be as follows: Donnie Sumner would get a phone call informing him Elvis was headed to his house in Palm Springs, California, and wanted the group to come out. "Catch a flight, get to Palm Springs tomorrow, check into the Hilton, and wait for a phone call." They would do as directed, and maybe around eight or nine o'clock in the evening the phone would ring in their hotel. "Elvis is up and around; he'll probably want to sing some. Come on out to the house." They would load up, go to the gate, clear security, and go into the house.

As an entertainer, Elvis was notoriously a night person. His "working" hours were flip-flopped from the familiar, get-up-in-the-morning-and-go-to-work routine most of us know; instead, Elvis would sing all night, or practice karate and have karate demonstrations, watch movies, or engage people in conversations on various topics. This was his time to unwind and spend time with the people he liked. He'd go to bed in the morning, sleep most of the day, if he was able to sleep, and rise the next evening to start the cycle all over.

The members of Voice had the rare opportunity to see Elvis when he wasn't in the limelight. "He was just a normal person, a nice person," Tony Brown said. Sometimes he would take some of the guys shopping with him, along with Red or Sonny or some of his other bodyguards. "Sometimes I'd hear him humming one of the old songs," Tony said, "and that was my cue to run to the piano and figure out what key he was in. Everybody would come around the piano and we'd start singing." Elvis didn't want to sing "Jailhouse Rock" or any of those songs; he wanted to sing "The Old, Rugged Cross," or "Nearer, My God, to Thee," or "He Touched Me," or one of his other gospel favorites.

Chapter Seven

FOR THE LOVE OF MUSIC

No one long survives the physical, mental, and emotional grind of the entertainment industry unless possessed of an innate and sincere love of the music. Elvis was a prime example; indeed, one of the things that made him so popular during his lifetime and beyond is, I believe, the passion for music and entertaining he was so readily able to communicate to his listeners, both live and those who bought his recordings.

Those of us who worked with him never ceased to be astonished by the depth and breadth of his knowledge. He had a vast record collection and none of it gathered dust. He knew every artist, every recording, and nearly every live performance. Not only did he know the songs, he knew the interplay of the parts. He could tell me, for example, on a particular song recorded by The Imperials, when the lead switched from one singer to another, how that was different from one or more previous tracks, and several other pertinent factors I might not have noticed myself—even though I was one of the performers! He remembered who recorded what and when, and he wasn't hesitant about sharing his knowledge.

Jake Hess recalls a break during a gospel recording session when he sat with Elvis and talked for a long time about the history of gospel music. Elvis admitted to Hess that his true life's ambition was to become a gospel performer. "Well, why don't you do it?" Hess asked him. In a poignant reply, typical of his sense of responsibility for those around him, Elvis stated, "No, look at the thousands of people who'd be out of work if I did that." Realizing his pop star status had built an almost industrial infrastructure about him, an infrastructure supporting so many, Elvis must have felt, in some measure, trapped by his success— or at least that it had become a barrier between himself and his deepest aspirations.

Still, he had the ability to throw himself wholeheartedly into the music, whether the setting was the recording studio, the stage, or a private gathering with friends. And his enthusiasm never waned. Often one of us would hear a song we thought he'd like, and we'd play it for him. He'd listen to it, and if it connected with him, he might play the record a hundred times over the next week, absorbing the song as completely as he could. He would give special attention to songs a friend wrote—partly, I always thought, because of his instinctively generous nature. What songwriter wouldn't want Elvis Presley to do one of his songs? And Elvis accommodated, if there was any way possible.

In this connection, publishing rights for the songs were often the bone of contention, though not with Elvis; he distanced himself from such considerations. For him, it was all about the music and the way he responded to it. If something about the song captured his imagination, recording magic was usually the result. However, many of those around Elvis had more practical matters in mind, especially where the royalty-generating potential of a possible hit was concerned. If a particular song was pitched to Elvis by someone, that person might be asked to share writer and publisher credits with Elvis and his publishing company if the song made the album. Elvis just wanted to do the song, but others were more interested in the business side of things.

Certainly, Colonel Parker was very concerned with the publishing rights for everything Elvis did. Sometimes people thought they had a song on an album, only to find out later the song didn't get on because the deal couldn't be made with the Colonel, the writer, and/or the publisher.

Elvis was also generous in performance; it mattered little to him who was in the spotlight. At any given moment, he might focus everyone's attention on his backup singers, or on the guys in the TCB Band, or on somebody else onstage. For him, the important thing was the music—he did whatever it took to communicate that to the audience, and expected us to do the same. When he looked around, he wanted to see us nodding and smiling and supporting him. And, of course, his fans and his fellow performers loved him for it. I honestly believe that as long as you were doing your job as a musician, singer, and entertainer, Elvis believed you were just as important to the mix as he was. He was willing, even eager, to share his stage and his platform—an attribute not usually found in a big star.

Typical of this attitude is an instance when Bill Baize, one of the Stamps, was called out in the middle of the show to do a special number. Bill later went up to Elvis, deeply moved, and expressed his profound gratitude. "You're so big, Elvis," he said, "and I'm a nobody." Elvis' response? "I'm not so big—I'm only six-two," he said into Bill's ear as he hugged him. In other words, Elvis was acutely aware that he was only a human, and that his performance depended on the skill and dedication of his supporting cast. Knowing this with certainty only made us more intent on delivering the goods—no matter what the performance setting.

Most musicians who've been performing for any length of time have experienced those moments when everything works, when the sound, the connection, the meaning of the music takes on an almost physical presence in the room. Whether the medium is classical, country, jazz, pop, rock and roll, or gospel, these are the times you live for as a musician: those instants of knowing you've just taken part in creating something beautiful, or moving, or powerful—or all three. It's the ultimate payoff for any artist, a high so intense that once you've experienced it, you'd be willing to spend the rest of your life trying to duplicate it.

When that happened around Elvis, he would give a little shiver. "Whew!" someone would say, and then we'd all laugh. It was our way of acknowledging that instant of magic. For us, it was much like those moments in church when the preacher says something so moving and true all the people can do is say, "Amen!" The shiver and laugh was our "amen" to the music, to the perfection of the moment. It might come onstage as Elvis listened to the quartet singing "Sweet, Sweet Spirit," or it might happen in the suite with everyone gathered around the piano as Donnie Sumner sang the lead on "Lighthouse," one of Elvis' favorites. It was our applause not so much for ourselves as for the privilege of being able to do something worthwhile and beautiful—and the spirit among us that made it possible.

Maybe this is part of the reason Elvis' closest friends and associates were those of us who performed with him—along with his old friends and family members in the entourage, of course.

He never sought out the companionship of his fellow stars, or even the wealthy and famous people whom he invited to his suite after his shows. As I've said before, Elvis was *big*. An invitation to his suite after a show was the hot ticket. In fact, people would find excuses to hang around after the concert was over, hoping for an invitation to "the show after the show." I think he viewed those famous people very selectively; he would pick and choose which of them were afforded a chance to see "the real Elvis." Always, his most intimate trust was reserved for The Imperials, the Stamps, the Sweets, members of the TCB Band, and especially the intimate inner circle of family members and longtime cronies who lived with him and rarely left his side, who were sometimes referred to as the "Memphis Mafia." He was driven, energized, and passionate about his music, and the moments of greatest pleasure for him were centered on performing and listening to it. I think that's why he counted us as his friends.

Elvis' love and respect for his music was also demonstrated by the risks he would take, the things he would try. While we were with him, I observed time and again his unwillingness to rest on past successes. He would change something, do something differently, sing a phrase higher or lower than he'd ever done, always trying to push the envelope, to exploit every bit of emotional power the music contained, and then some. Even though we were seasoned performers, we were continually amazed by the depths into which he could reach, the way he always had a little more to give. As Terry Blackwood once said, you can't play it cool and maintain your distance from your material and bring that kind of power and freshness to every performance. I had the feeling Elvis was most alive when he was pouring out his heart into a song.

In rehearsals, Elvis would gather us around the piano and play individual parts as he envisioned them, going over and over again to make sure we understood what he wanted. Another amazing thing about Elvis was that he could remember lyrics better than anyone I ever saw. Most singers, especially in rehearsal or the recording studio, will at least use a word sheet, just to make sure they don't forget something. But Elvis could listen to a song one time—even one with complicated, dense lyrics like "Joshua Fit de Battle"—and nail every verse, every chorus, every vocal embellishment. He had a truly gifted memory. Others have commented on it, and I suppose that was just one more of the many attributes that made Elvis the incredible performer he was. He was an unbelievably quick study. This also stood him in good stead for his movies; he could learn a script for the day's shooting on the drive to the set.

Another thing that helped make Elvis a superstar had partly to do with the particular moment in American popular music when he arrived on the scene, and partly to do with his amazing ability to fuse different styles into something uniquely his own. This was Elvis' seemingly instinctive blending of African American, country, and early rock-and-roll influences. This is why artists like Elton John, Bruce Springsteen, and John Lennon have acknowledged the way Elvis stood like a bridge across several different musical streams. Or maybe he was less a bridge than some kind of huge channel, changing the direction of the flow from three separate streams into a single river.

Performers with roots in black gospel have said that when Elvis sang gospel, he affected them differently than most white performers did; it had more in common with the styles they were used to. In gospel, as with his rock-and-roll hits, it was Elvis' particular genius to be able to pull together different styles in order to bring to life the sound and energy he was able to visualize for the music.

"Before Elvis, there was nothing."

—*John Lennon*

Perhaps this unique approach, this willingness to borrow from different musical traditions and blur boundary lines, was part of what Elvis came to appreciate about our group, The Imperials. He certainly remained a fan of traditional Southern and African American gospel music, but he was also acutely aware of the changes taking place in Contemporary Christian Music, especially on the West Coast. Like Elvis, The Imperials were interested in building on the strengths of the Southern gospel quartet style but also incorporating the energy and immediacy of more contemporary stylistic influences.

Some of the impetus for this development came from the "Jesus music" of the mid-1960s, a fusion of gospel and rock that came of age during the days of social protest and the questioning of authority. As some began to seek more constructive solutions to the problems of society, Jesus' teachings about loving one's neighbor and seeking peace began to hold greater appeal. The music that evolved from this time in history reflects both the faith-based hopes sustaining Christians for centuries and the searching and challenging mind-set typical of the anti-war movement.

This can certainly be heard on the albums The Imperials produced in the mid- to late 1960s. On songs like "Gospel Ship," we were able to combine the close harmonies of quartet singing with the driving beat and rhythm section popular with fans of secular rock and roll. Our lyrics, of course, spoke of heaven, of placing trust in God, and of the importance of prayer and reflective living. A song like Andrae Crouch's "I've Got Confidence" is another great example of the way different influences came together, both in the music of The Imperials and of Elvis. Sherman Andrus, who came to The Imperials from Andrae Crouch and the Disciples, brought this particular song to our attention, and we subsequently recorded it. Elvis loved it, and decided he wanted to include it on *He Touched Me*. The song, a jubilant, lively tune about faith, has obvious African American gospel origins, but the two-stepping beat of the chorus almost resembles an up-tempo country song.

Elvis was so certain of where he wanted to go musically that I've wondered if he would even have thought of what we were doing as "contemporary," or of using any other label. It was as simple as this: If he liked a song and could visualize himself doing it and bringing something fresh to it, he would incorporate it. This may account for the fact that on his last gospel album, *He Touched Me*, six or seven of the songs were pieces The Imperials put on our most recent record. When it came time to record, it was pretty simple: we just stepped back and let Elvis sing lead on substantially the same arrangements we'd just finished recording. He already knew them all.

In 1971, The Imperials were doing around 250 dates a year on our own, as a contemporary gospel group, as well as putting out a couple of albums per year. Elvis had all our albums, and he wanted to hear the new things we were doing as well. He was invigorated by both the approach and the arrangements, and our resulting work with him led to our opportunity to perform as his backup singers in the late 1960s and early 1970s.

Even after we left him, though, Elvis kept up with what we were doing. I remember one amusing incident—well, at least it was amusing to me—that happened when The Imperials were back in Las Vegas in 1972, working with Jimmy Dean at the Landmark Hotel. We found ourselves with an empty spot; we were a voice short on the baritone part, and as we tried to figure out how to replace a singer on such short notice, we remembered a guy we'd known for years we met during our swings through Texas. He was a law school student at that time, and his name was Larry Gatlin.

Larry was a big fan of gospel music. In fact, he, his brothers, and their mother sometimes appeared at our concerts as an opening act, with Mrs. Gatlin playing piano and the boys singing. Larry came to lots of our shows; I suppose he was a bit persistent and a bit on the overzealous side. He was constantly telling us how he knew all our songs, admired us, and wanted more than anything to be "in the business." Well, this seemed like a good opportunity for us to see if Larry was serious. We got hold of him, explained the situation, and asked if there was any way he could come to Vegas to fill in while we searched for a permanent baritone singer, a position that would later be filled by Sherman Andrus. The next thing we knew, Larry was in Vegas running through the show and learning the baritone part.

One night, during Jimmy Dean's show, some guy sitting at one of the tables in the back started making noise. Now, overzealous fans, and even hecklers, are not uncommon, and every entertainer has ways of dealing with the situation and moving ahead with the show, but this guy was really something else. "Let The Imperials sing!" he hollered, over and over. He just would not be quiet. Eventually, Jimmy Dean reached his limit. "Give me a spotlight on that guy's table," he said from the stage, and when the beam of light found the heckler, it turned out to be Elvis Presley.

He had closed his show at the International across the street and come over to the Landmark with a couple of his guys, slipping in after the house was darkened. Elvis decided he wanted to hear some gospel, so he started hollering for The Imperials. Jimmy Dean put as good a face on it as he could—he had Elvis stand up and wave to the crowd, passed the whole thing off with a joke or two, and I think we did actually sing a couple of gospel numbers so Elvis would let Jimmy get on with the rest of his show. After the show, of course, Elvis came backstage. He was wearing his "heavyweight champion" buckle, presented to him by the City of Las Vegas in recognition of the record-breaking attendance at his shows. Larry grinned from ear to ear. Larry and his brothers, of course, went on to become stars in their own right as Larry Gatlin and the Gatlin Brothers, composing and performing many hits and selling a lot of records. I'm pretty sure Larry never finished law school.

As it does in so many marriages, the pressure of career concerns began to erode Elvis and Priscilla's relationship. The constant traveling and media exposure would have been difficult enough, but Elvis' deep need to perform and record, to be searching constantly for new and better means of musical self-expression, only added to the conflict between them. Near the end of 1971, Priscilla moved out of Graceland, taking three-year-old Lisa Marie with her.

Elvis was publicly gracious about the separation and eventual divorce. In at least one concert setting, he introduced Priscilla to the audience and asserted that he bore the blame for the split, due to the constant pressures of his career. But privately, Elvis never really got over the divorce. There would be other women in his life, for sure, but I believe he regarded the loss of his marriage as one of the greatest failures of his life. In many ways, it was a blow from which he never recovered.

Chapter Eight

STIRRINGS IN THE SOUL

Everyone needs a challenge in life, something to strive toward and look forward to with anticipation. This was certainly true for Elvis Presley. I believe that, like most of us, he was at his best when facing a new opportunity, a chance for growth and personal development. In the early years, simply the prospect of being able to have his music heard by the public energized and motivated him. When that dream came true, his aspirations increased toward the goal of extending his popularity beyond Memphis and the South. As that goal, in turn, became a reality and his reputation and image continued to expand, he became interested in making movies. Then, later, with his return to live performance, he strove to give one hundred percent to each performance, to consolidate his loyal fan base and add new admirers.

The record of Elvis' achievement is truly remarkable; his list of "firsts" and "mosts" is probably without parallel in music and entertainment history. However, his personality and makeup were such that the very pursuit of his dreams locked him into a sort of cycle: as each goal was reached, Elvis realized its attainment left a void. *What is next?* he must have wondered. *What is left to try?* It was during these times, I think, his spiritual searching, his need to discover answers to the deep questions of life, became most acute. It was also during these times, I suspect, that his tendency to rely on temporary "fixes" was most difficult for him to resist.

After our time performing with Elvis came to an end, The Imperials went on with a busy schedule of touring, concerts, recording, and television network appearances. We had the opportunity to work with Jimmy Dean and other big-name stars, and things were generally going well. Still, as I continued to have occasional contact with Elvis, it seemed to me he wasn't looking well—and he certainly didn't seem happy.

Not too long after this, I began to feel a tug in my own heart, a conviction that I needed to do something, as Elvis' friend, to be supportive of him and of the ideals I knew he had for himself. Kenneth Taylor's paraphrase version of the Bible, *The Living Bible*, had been published not long before, and I was an admirer of its simple, straightforward language. I began to think that one of these Bibles would be a great gift for Elvis. I knew he was an avid reader, and I remembered how many times the discussions we had turned on biblical themes. Maybe a Bible that was easy to read and understand would be something in which he could find comfort and guidance, I thought.

In May of 1975, he was appearing in Huntsville, Alabama, only about a two-hour drive from Nashville. I drove down and all during the trip I was trying to decide what I'd say if I got the chance to talk to Elvis. I wanted to just be a friend, to encourage him. As I thought about this, I realized this was a different position for me to be in—me, offering encouragement to Elvis Presley? He had done so much for me, both professionally and personally—he was one of the world's biggest superstars, and I was trying to offer something to him? Still, I really felt this was something I had to do, or at least attempt.

I went to the show and was able to talk to some of the guys in the entourage. They must have told him I was there because someone came back to me and said, "E wants you to drop by the hotel after the show." So far, so good, I thought.

After the concert I went to the hotel and was cleared past security. I went up to Elvis' floor, and the party was already in progress. I visited with some people, but soon noticed Elvis was nowhere to be seen. I asked Sonny about it and was told he was tired and had not come out of his bedroom yet. Sonny told me I could go in and see Elvis, so I went to his room, and sure enough, he was in his pajamas. He seemed glad to see me; it had been awhile since we last had a chance to visit. We chatted for a while and exchanged a few stories.

He didn't look good to me; he appeared puffy and physically worn down. His color didn't seem right, somehow. I remember I was a bit taken aback by his overall appearance.

Then I handed Elvis the Bible. I'd written a simple inscription inside the front cover: *To Elvis*. I told him I knew he was sincerely searching for something in his life that he hadn't found. In all of the books he was reading, all the people he was talking to, all the spiritual and intellectual theories he was studying, I told him, I knew he was looking for stability, for some source of peace. In my mind, it seemed so simple. So I said, "Elvis, all of the answers you're looking for are right here in this book. Just read it."

He opened the cover and read the inscription, and then he did something I'd never experienced before. Usually with Elvis, it was always just a handshake. He wasn't really overly demonstrative physically. Some men hug, and some shake hands, some pat you on the back—Elvis was usually content with a simple handshake. But this time, he reached out his arm and cupped the back of my head, then pulled me close to his face. He squeezed our foreheads together in a sort of embrace and he said, "Thanks, Joe. This means a lot to me."

Not too long after this, another event took place that had profound implications for Elvis' life. Rex Humbard and his wife, Maude Aimee, were vacationing in Las Vegas, staying at Caesars Palace. They called their friend James Blackwood and asked if he knew of a way they could get tickets to see Elvis' show. James, in turn, called J.D., and soon the Humbards had front-row seats for the dinner show, which they enjoyed very much.

Elvis, of course, knew they were there, and wanted a chance to speak with these people whose ministry he had admired for so long. He invited them back to his dressing room after the show.

"Elvis, I want you to know I've been praying for you for years," Maude Aimee Humbard said a few minutes into the visit. "You're my bell sheep."

Elvis was puzzled by this terminology, and asked for an explanation. Rex explained to him that shepherds in the Holy Land often tied a bell around the neck of one of the sheep. The rest of the flock would follow wherever they were led by the sound of the bell.

"Elvis," Maude Aimee went on, "I've been praying that you'll have a spiritual experience that will cause you to lead thousands of people to the Lord."

At that point, something began happening inside Elvis. Rex related later that he began to shake; tears began rolling down his cheeks. The Humbards prayed with Elvis. It was a moment of profound spiritual experience for all three of them.

A moment later, Lisa Marie Presley, who happened to be visiting her father, came into the room. "Why is my daddy crying?" she wanted to know.

"It's all right, honey," Elvis told her, gently stroking her hair. "Everything is fine." When the Humbards tried to leave, knowing that many other people were waiting to speak to Elvis, he begged them to stay. Clearly, something was happening that he was hoping to prolong; he found a place of respite apparently long absent despite his searching and reading, his questioning into all sorts of different spiritual paths. I believe that, in those moments with the Humbards, Elvis was brought back to what he had known from his earliest days. I suspect that in Maude Aimee's words he heard echoes of his mother's voice and was reminded of the teaching he'd received as a boy in Tupelo.

I wish I could tell you that there was some kind of dramatic turnaround in his life when I gave Elvis the Bible—or when the Humbards visited him, for that matter. I wish I could say he went on from there and never again used any artificial "crutches" to give himself some sort of temporary relief from the thoughts troubling him so. But the record is pretty clear that no dramatic turnaround happened. About all I can say is I did what I knew to do at the time, what I felt in my heart I had to do—and I did it with every good wish and intention in the world. I'm sure the Humbards felt the same way.

. . . .

NOT LONG AGO, I gained an important insight into what was going through Elvis' mind and heart during his last couple of years. In Jerry Osborne's *Elvis: Word for Word*, I found transcriptions of some notes Elvis apparently wrote to himself during a December 1976 run at the Las Vegas Hilton (the International was bought by the Hilton hotel chain in 1971). The first is dated December 7:

> I feel so alone sometimes . . . The night is quiet for me . . . I would love to be able to sleep . . . I'm glad everyone is gone now . . . I will probably not rest tonight . . . I have no need for all this . . . Help me, Lord . . .

The second note is even more heart-wrenching; it reveals a man who feels isolated, even though he is among close associates. And yet, Elvis shows evidence of clinging to his faith, if seemingly in growing desperation:

> I don't know who I can talk to anymore. Nor to turn to. I only have myself and the Lord. Help me, Lord, to know the right thing.

Finally, a similar note expresses many of the same sentiments, yet also concludes with words of faith:

> I wish there was someone who I could trust and talk to. Prayer is my only salvation now. I feel lost sometimes. . . . Be still and *know I am God* [original is underlined]. Feel me within, before you know *I am there* [original underlined].

As I read these records of Elvis' private thoughts, I was moved to deep sorrow for this man whom I admired so much and considered a friend. Without question, some of his isolation and feelings of confusion were the consequence of actions that were the result of poor decisions or negative habits. And yet, I can't help finding a sad irony in knowing that this man, whose aim in life was to entertain and bring enjoyment to his audiences, was, at the end, feeling so bereft of human understanding and fellowship.

"He was an intensely lonely person, so alone with his fame and his thoughts."

—T. G. Sheppard

From my perspective, Elvis suffered three major depressive episodes in his life, all triggered or worsened by traumatic events. The first was when his mother died. The second was when he and Priscilla divorced, and the third was close to the end, when Red West, Sonny West, and Dave Hebler left his employ and wrote their book.

I've often thought his despondency over his mother's passing may have contributed to Elvis' merry-go-round use of uppers to keep him going and sleeping pills to relax him when he needed rest. Unfortunately, this went on for most of the rest of his life.

As for the divorce from Priscilla, this, too, was an event that rocked Elvis' world down to its very foundations. As anyone can attest who has had a marriage fall apart, divorce is never easy or without negative consequences. It isn't necessary to assign blame to any party to know divorce creates many varieties of misery for any person involved—sometimes unforeseen misery and sometimes misery that lasts for decades after the dry legalities are concluded. There is no question in my mind that Elvis and Priscilla truly loved each other, but the time came when that love just wasn't enough. It's impossible for any of us even to try to imagine the pressures and strains this relationship had to withstand. How unfortunate—for both Elvis and Priscilla. The pain of the divorce took its toll on Elvis as he continued to immerse himself in what was seemingly his only escape.

In some ways, I don't think Elvis ever fully came to terms with the death of his dream of a happy family. Elvis tried to medicate his pain over the divorce in several ways, I think, but not in ways that proved positive for his long-term physical or emotional health. And then, to add to his heartache, his career and the security of the isolated life he built was starting to change in ways that would take an additional toll.

As Elvis entered this downward spiral, those around him did their best to take care of him in the only ways they knew how: they tried to keep him busy, tried to keep him occupied, tried to help him focus on his concert and recording work, tried to do anything they could that seemed to help him move forward rather than sinking into the pit looming larger and larger in his life. Inevitably, as everyone did everything in his or her power to take care of Elvis, competing agendas came to the fore. Sometimes this resulted in access to Elvis being restricted to only a handful of persons. Sometimes it resulted in angry differences of opinion between close friends and family members. Eventually, such differences of opinion caused Vernon Presley to tell Red and Sonny West they were no longer part of Elvis' organization. They were fired, along with karate instructor Dave Hebler.

Red, Sonny, and Dave responded by writing a book, *Elvis, What Happened?*, revealing their accounts of many unfortunate experiences with Elvis. They have stated they hoped seeing some of his dark moments in print would shock Elvis into a different way of living—a more balanced, constructive way. Whether the book might have had such an effect may never be known, since Elvis passed soon after the book's release. Still, his sadness over this rift with lifelong friends, it seems to me, propelled him deeper into the darkness swirling around him in his final days.

My deepest regret during this time is that many of us who cared deeply about Elvis were unable, for various reasons, to reach out to him as effectively as we would have wished—and the worst part was that we didn't know why. Changes were going on we didn't know about, since we were only part of his music world and not involved in his personal affairs.

Elvis even lost his desire to sing gospel, the only gift many of us had to offer him. This, in itself, indicates how great his misery must have been, since even his beloved gospel music seemed to have little remaining value for him.

Even though I experienced it from a distance, it was perhaps the greatest tragedy I've ever had to witness in my lifetime. It saddens me to this day.

Chapter Nine

AUGUST 18, 1977

August in Memphis: The sun bears down on you like a physical weight; the humidity combines with the heat to create a stifling atmosphere making it hard to think about anything except how to cool off. The sweat seeps from every pore of your skin; asphalt bubbles up through the cracks of streets that have been transformed into solar heat panels. Even the leaves on the trees hang limp. You pray for a breeze, a patch of shade. You remember how grateful you are to live in the age of air conditioning.

That's how it was when we got to Graceland for Elvis' funeral. And as if the heat weren't enough to contend with, a heavy mantle of grief lay over us all, adding to the burden each of us carried.

I was working for BMI in Nashville at the time. On the sixteenth, I got a call from a friend named Bill Hance, who was a staff writer for the evening newspaper in Nashville, the *Banner*. Bill was talking so fast I couldn't understand him at first:

"It just came over the wire," he stammered. Elvis had died at Graceland.

Shocked, I immediately called Priscilla and found out that she and Lisa Marie were just leaving to meet the plane Vernon was sending to bring the West Coast family and friends back to Memphis. My wife and I were close friends with Priscilla at the time; I hadn't been traveling or working with Elvis since the end of 1971, so we were coming down to Memphis at Priscilla's request, to be part of her support group. I remember the four-hour drive from Nashville to Memphis that day with my wife, each of us in our own separate fog of sorrow. We never spoke a word to each other; we listened to the radio all the way down. Elvis' death was all any station was talking about, along with solid marathons of nothing but his music. It was weird—surreal, in a way.

We went straight to Graceland to meet Priscilla, and she arranged for us to stay with a couple of her very close friends. Everyone was handling the news in his or her own way: some were in total shock, walking around with a dazed look; some cried incessantly; and some of us just wanted to keep busy. Friends and family were pouring in from every direction.

Vernon looked to me like a broken man. He asked J. D. Sumner to help him put his son's service together, and they met in Charlie Hodge's room to plan and work out the details. Charlie, however, was not much help; he was one of the incessant criers. J.D. basically took charge and started to call the gospel music community together to take part in the service, to sing E's favorite songs one more time. He and Vernon decided to call on Rex Humbard to speak, in addition to the minister of a local Church of Christ.

As you walked around inside Graceland, you would see two or three people huddled in a corner, telling their favorite Elvis story or sharing their fondest memory. Everyone there was visibly shaken in some unique way. Some looked out the windows at the throng of fans gathered at the gate. I also remember the smell of home cooking wafting from the kitchen. As anyone knows who has ever been to a family funeral in the South, there's always a big meal, either before or after the service. The Graceland kitchen staff was making sure there would be plenty of Elvis' favorites available for his guests: pork chops, mashed potatoes, meat loaf, buttermilk cornbread, peach cobbler, and other traditional mainstays of Southern cuisine.

During the afternoon of the day before the funeral, the security staff was instructed to open the gates and allow people to file past the casket, which was on display in the foyer. Vernon insisted on allowing the fans to come up the driveway to the front door of Graceland and view the body. They couldn't stop, and for the rest of the afternoon the silent procession approached the house, two by two, in a polite and adoring way. There were thousands of them, and even though the security staff extended the viewing time, it wasn't possible to accommodate everyone who wanted to see the body. At the end, there were still maybe ten thousand people standing outside the gate, hoping to see Elvis' casket. The guards were able to get the gates closed without incident, though for a while it was touch and go.

The day of Elvis' funeral was another day of many overwhelming impressions. Like many across the nation, I'll never forget seeing the crowds of people outside the gates of Graceland, standing in the searing sun as they demonstrated their grief over Elvis' sudden loss. The florists in Memphis reportedly ran out of flowers and had to send out far and wide to fulfill all their orders. There were some of the most amazing floral construc-tions I've ever seen—masterpieces, I would say. It took nearly four hours to deliver all the arrangements to the cemetery.

I remember thinking that this looked like a scene of national mourning, and I guess that's exactly what it was: the whole nation was mourning the loss of an original, a one-of-a-kind personality whose like would never be seen again. From the crowds and the whole atmosphere you would have thought a president or some other head of state had died.

Graceland, like most mansions built in the antebellum style, had a living room to the right of the entry foyer. Another room lay off the living room: Elvis called it the music room, and it held his white baby-grand piano. Straight ahead when you walk in the front door is a staircase, and a dining room lay to the left. All that space was filled with people invited to attend the funeral: friends and family, of course, but also too many celebrities to mention. Caroline Kennedy was there, though only a young girl at the time. People were crammed inside the house to pay their final respects to the man who made it all possible. The family was seated in the living room, closest to the casket, and the musicians were in the music room, gathered near the piano, along with those officiating the service.

By the time the service began, it was decided that instead of the Stamps singing a song, or The Imperials, or any of the other groups, the singers would be mixed. That seemed proper to us; we had all known him, worked with him, and seen our lives changed forever by the experience. It was better we show him this last honor not as the Stamps, The Imperials, the Jorda-naires, the Blackwoods, or the Statesmen, but together around the piano, mixing our voices as we sang the songs he loved most during his life—those we sang with him.

To be honest, many of the details have faded in my memory, maybe because I don't really enjoy thinking about that day. But I do remember Jake Hess sang "Known Only to Him." What powerful words! I think I really heard them for the first time that day: "Known only to him are the great hidden secrets. . . . I fear not the darkness when my path grows dim." Amazing, even now, as I remember it. Jake sang the song with such feeling, it seemed as if he were singing it straight to Elvis and allowing us all to listen in. Everyone was touched and moved by this beautiful song.

Kathy Westmoreland sang "Heavenly Father," accompanied by Hovie Lister. James Blackwood sang "How Great Thou Art," and Joe Guercio stood to one side and conducted one last time, as he had so many times onstage. This time, though, there were tears streaming down his face. As James sang, you could see people throughout the crowd moving their lips to the words of this hymn that was so connected in our minds with Elvis' memory.

"Now that he's gone, I find it more helpful to remember his good qualities, and I hope you do, too."
—from the funeral sermon by C. W. Bradley

Jackie Kahane, the comedian who performed on the Vegas shows, gave a brief, informal eulogy, talking about how a sense of family developed among all the performers and crew. Rex Humbard spoke of the meeting in Las Vegas where he and Maude Aimee had prayed with Elvis, and of the matters they discussed at that time. Then the minister of the Wooddale Church of Christ, C. W. Bradley, gave the main sermon, focusing on Elvis' basic decency and generosity. He spoke about his determination to succeed, and how, rather than focusing on his negative qualities, we should be inspired by his good ones.

At the end of the service, everyone filed past the casket for a final good-bye. The pallbearers—Billy and Gene Smith, Joe Esposito, Charlie Hodge, Felton Jarvis, Lamar Fike, Jerry Schilling, George Klein, and Dr. George Nichopoulos—moved the casket into the white hearse that would lead the procession of seventeen white limos the three and a half miles from Graceland to Forest Hill Cemetery. It took us over an hour to cover the short distance because fifteen to twenty thousand people were lining the way, wanting a last point of contact with Elvis. The crowd included people from every walk of life: old and young, rich and poor, white and black. There were bikers and people pushing baby strollers. As I think about it, it was like the typical crowd at one of his shows, lining the street. It was the most amazing cross-section of humanity you can imagine, and they were all drawn together by their love of Elvis' music and their fascination with his image.

So, you see, even at the end, it was gospel music that accompanied the passing of Elvis Presley. The same music that comforted him and his family at his mother's funeral now rang in our ears and our hearts as we escorted to its final resting place the body of this man who shared his heart with the world.

Epilogue

THE LAST THIRTY YEARS

W as Elvis chosen? Was he, in some way, anointed, selected for a special role or fate even he couldn't guess?
I suppose very few days have gone by during the last thirty years
when I haven't thought about Elvis in some way. After all, I'm
deeply involved, as are others, in Elvis commemorations of various types, in fan club activities both in this country and abroad,
in concerts and promotional activities. For the past ten years,
I've been a part of *Elvis: The Concert*, a live event that features
Elvis on a thirty-foot Jumbotron screen accompanied by live
musicians like myself who've actually toured and performed
with him. This event premiered at the Mid-South Coliseum in
Memphis in connection with the twentieth anniversary of Elvis'
death, and played again at the Pyramid in Memphis for the
twenty-fifth anniversary. This show plays to sell-out crowds all
over the world, and is scheduled to appear at the FedEx Forum
in August 2007 in connection with the thirtieth anniversary. On
Sirius satellite radio, channel 13 is "all Elvis, all the time." The
twice-annual pilgrimage to Memphis by thousands of fans, the

candlelight vigils outside the gates of Graceland each August that seem to grow each year—does any of this sound like a fading trend? I don't think so. As you can see, I have ample reasons to ponder Elvis and the almost unbelievable fascination he holds for people—even thirty years after his death.

What was so special about him? What made him "work" for so many people, then and now? Part of the answer, I think, lies in his personal charisma. When you were in Elvis' presence, you had no choice but to be drawn in. Time and again, people who were near him have spoken of the way he could engage you and just not let go. If he really wanted to, he could talk you into anything—a trait that could, admittedly, be both good and bad. He was so sincere, so transparent, even in his flaws, people were simply disarmed. Even Hollywood producers and executives, who survive by retaining a healthy sense of cynicism, were charmed by Elvis' politeness, his consideration of others' feelings, and his wish to please. Most people just don't expect such traits in a superstar.

I don't want to get carried away here, but I think Elvis' personal magnetism could be compared to that of some of the most brilliant and influential leaders the world has ever known. In fact, I think you'd almost have to go outside the music and entertainment world to find a single person who has had a more sweeping impact on culture. As I said earlier, the "Elvis" figure is one of the most recognizable images worldwide—easily as much so as a corporate logo like Coca-Cola's. In fact, the federal laws governing the protection of images and likenesses were changed and strengthened as a result of efforts by Elvis' estate, a change that has benefited artists ever since. Consider this: Elvis earned some $50 million last year—more than he ever made in a single year when he was alive! His recordings generate more sales now than ever; each year his music outsells that of most other recording artists. His movies, TV specials, concert documentaries, and the products based on these continue to be rebroadcast, repackaged, and remarketed every year. He has 500 fan clubs worldwide—and that's just counting the "official" ones. And his audiences continue to grow: half of the audience members for *Elvis: The Concert* are under thirty-five—hardly confined to baby boomers!

It gets embarrassing sometimes. I can make a factual statement of some kind in a crowd of Elvis enthusiasts and be immediately contradicted by someone—and the person will be correct! I was there, and I don't know as much about what happened as some of the fans who have researched relentlessly, reading every thing they can get their hands on, eager to know everything they can about every aspect of Elvis Presley's life and work. In fact, I've learned over the years to speak in generalities during the question-and-answer sessions following many of the Elvis events in which I participate each year. Just let me or someone sharing the stage with me make a misstatement about a recording session, for example, and someone among the fans gathered will say, "Ah, excuse me, Joe, but that session was actually in July at RCA Studios in Nashville, and the session musicians playing on it were . . ." Elvis fans are some of the best-informed people in the world, whether I'm in Brazil, Japan, or the United States. The world's fascination with this man just continues to live on and on. His influence just keeps increasing; he is more relevant today than ever.

In 1999, Elvis' name was mentioned as a possibility for induction into the Gospel Music Hall of Fame. At the time, I asked, somewhat jokingly, "Is he eligible?" In order to be considered for induction, a person must have had a minimum of twenty-five years' association with gospel music. As the conversation progressed, we began to realize that, indeed, Elvis' work certainly met that requirement. After all, his first gospel recording was released in 1957. There was no question of his fulfilling the history requirement. Elvis was nominated and placed on the ballot, and subsequently elected. I was honored, along with Gordon Stoker of the Jordanaires and Ed Enoch of the Stamps, to present this award, which was accepted by Jack Soden, chief executive officer of Elvis Presley Enterprises, on behalf of the Presley estate. I imagine that Elvis would have been prouder of this honor than almost any other he received during his lifetime: to be recognized by the gospel music industry for his accomplishments in the style nearest his heart—I think he just might have been speechless.

Here's what I said on this memorable occasion:

Standing here, we represent a small part of the singers and musicians who worked with Elvis through the years, both in the studio and on personal appearances. We say thank you for that privilege and for exposing us and our music to an audience who might not have ever heard of gospel music. Thank you to the great Gordon Stoker and all the Jordanaires, Jake Hess and all The Imperials, to J. D. Sumner and all the Stamps Quartet members, and to all the Sweet Inspirations, who always added so much to his personal appearances.

To us it seems fitting and proper that this [tribute] has been accomplished. Elvis would be so proud of this honor. Elvis was a student and fan of gospel music. He loved it. He knew every word, every song, every song-writer, every arrangement. He knew each one of you by name and what part you sang, and could sing right along with you. His gospel music collection was quite extensive, and he would listen for hours to Monty and Bill Matthews, the Foggy River Boys, Jimmy Jones and the Harmonizing Four, the Golden Gate Quartet, the Blackwoods and Statesmen, the Speer Family, the Bill Gaither Trio, and so many more. He admired you and respected you.

We would like to thank the Gospel Music Association, its board of directors, and the GMA Gospel Music Hall of Fame Committee for recognizing his contribution to gospel music and for bestowing this honor on our friend, Elvis Aaron Presley.

Who could ever have imagined what has transpired over the thirty years since Elvis died? Who could have possibly anticipated the way the shadow cast by his life and work has continued to grow? And the amazing thing is plans are underway to extend his legacy further for years to come.

Of course, none of this would have happened without the dedication and foresight of people like Priscilla, Lisa Marie, Gary Hovey, and Jack Soden, who have exercised careful stewardship over the vast and rich artistic heritage Elvis left behind. The driving force behind their combined vision was the determination that things would be done right.

I recall visiting with Priscilla in 1979, before Graceland was officially opened to the public, when an offer from the State of Tennessee was made to the estate and the board to take over

Graceland as a public attraction—much like a state park. Priscilla and I discussed this offer and I am so proud of her insistence on keeping Graceland in the hands and under the direct control of the family and the Presley estate. Graceland has become what it is today due to her compassion, leadership, and insight. There were so many decisions to be made at that time, and this one has proven overwhelmingly positive for Elvis fans and the preservation of his music and memory.

Remember, too, that all of this took place before the advent of the Internet. Who could have possibly dreamed of the way the worldwide information revolution would guarantee the instantaneous, global dissemination of Elvis to a data-hungry public? In fact, sometime when you've got several hours to spend, key "Elvis Presley" into your favorite Internet search engine and browse the results. A friend told me that the last time he tried it, he got just over 4.4 million hits in about a third of a second.

Of course, there was a "network" already in place in those early days, though it wasn't strictly computer-based. There were Elvis Presley fan clubs all over the world, thanks to the efforts of Colonel Parker; he always had friends and associates around the world for whom he would do special favors in return for promotion efforts—even though Elvis would never perform outside the United States during his lifetime. After Elvis' death, these efforts ramped up the intensity until we've now reached the point where promotion of Elvis is a worldwide cottage industry. There are fan clubs all over the world making money by selling merchandise and sponsoring concerts and special shows in their countries, along with other events throughout the year. There are thousands of Elvis impersonators in all sizes and shapes, singing Elvis' songs in dozens of languages around the globe. Each year in January (Birthday Week) and August, fans from all over the world descend on Memphis. There are also special fan club meetings at these times. These devout fans and enterprising businesspeople are a vital link in keeping Elvis in front of the public, and I'd especially like to mention David Wade and Keith Harris from England, Peter Verbruggen of Belgium, and Kathleen De-Nike. Of course, there are so many more—literally, thousands—who dedicate themselves to the preservation of Elvis' memory. The combined marketing, licensing, and promotional activities around the world are truly a phenomenon; as I mentioned above, each year the earnings of the Presley estate top the charts, even surpassing many artists still living and pounding the highways.

When Graceland officially opened its doors to the public in 1982, no one had any idea of the potential. Now, of course, we know that over 600,000 people visit Graceland each year, coming from all over the world. And with all the exciting new plans coming into view, the growth seems poised to continue.

Each year, Priscilla and Lisa Marie send out a holiday message to fans and special friends of Elvis. In the 2006 letter, they listed many exciting events, including the tribute paid to Elvis by the final four contestants of *American Idol.* Also, Graceland received a National Historic Landmark designation, as well as a visit to Graceland from President and Mrs. Bush and their guest, Prime Minister Koizumi of Japan, who happens to be a serious Elvis fan. Priscilla and Lisa Marie informed fans that 2007 would mark, in addition to the thirtieth anniversary of Elvis' death, the fiftieth anniversary of his purchase of Graceland, and the twenty-fifth anniversary of its opening to the public.

As I close this personal tribute to Elvis, I can't help but say it again: Who could have ever imagined all this? I'm certain Elvis would never have foreseen any of it. How could that shy young guy walking in off the street to Sun Studios back in 1953, paying his own hard-earned money to buy enough studio time to record a couple of songs, have guessed people around the world would still be talking about him, studying him, watching his videos, and writing books about him over a half century later? No, though he was certainly intelligent, Elvis Presley wasn't smart enough to have planned all this. Even the formidable Colonel Parker, with all his acumen, couldn't have imagined the imprint his "boy" would leave behind.

Today, there are only a handful of us left: those of us who lived with him, worked with him, made music with him, or shared his stage. But for any of us—or even beyond that, for any of those who acted with him, worked behind a camera or a light board when he was on a movie set, watched him through the glass of a recording control room, or had anything to do with his career, no matter how peripheral—the mention of his name is enough to bring a smile and, as often as not, a tear. It's been a thrill and a blessing for me to have been involved over the last thirty years, bringing Elvis Presley's life and music before an adoring public. And the deepest joy for me still comes in the chance to expose the world to his love for the music I fell in love with all those years ago.

Because the simple fact is this: You can't love the man as he really was until you've seen the gospel side of Elvis.

Appendix A

Gospel and Inspirational Songs Recorded and/or Performed by Elvis Presley (Excludes Christmas songs. All Songs are RCA.)

SONG (COMPOSER), YEAR RECORDED ALBUM

1. Amazing Grace (Newton), 1971 — *He Touched Me*

2. American Trilogy (Newbury), 1972 — *Aloha from Hawaii*

3. An Evening Prayer (Battersby, Gabriel), 1971 — *He Touched Me*

4. A Thing Called Love (Reed), 1971 — *He Touched Me*

5. Blessed Jesus (Hold My Hand) (trad.), 1956 — *The Million Dollar Quartet*

6. Bosom of Abraham (trad.), 1971 — *Amazing Grace*

7. Bridge over Troubled Water (Simon), 1970 — *That's the Way It Is*

SONG (COMPOSER), YEAR RECORDED ALBUM

8. By and By (trad.), 1966 — *How Great Thou Art*

9. Crying in the Chapel (Glenn), 1960 — single, A-side (*His Hand in Mine* sessions)

10. Down by the Riverside/When the Saints Go Marching In (trad.), 1956 — *The Million Dollar Quartet*

11. Farther Along (Stone), 1966 — *How Great Thou Art*

12. He Is My Everything (Frazier), 1971 — *He Touched Me*

13. He Knows Just What I Need (M. Lister), 1960 — *His Hand in Mine*

14. Help Me (Gatlin), 1971 — *Live on Stage in Memphis*

15. He Touched Me (Gaither), 1971 — *He Touched Me*

16. His Hand in Mine (M. Lister), 1960 — *His Hand in Mine*

17. How Great Thou Art (Hine), 1966 — *How Great Thou Art*

18. I Believe (Drake, Graham, Shirl, Stillman), 1957 — *Peace in the Valley*

19. I Believe in the Man in the Sky (Howard), 1960 — *His Hand in Mine*

20. If I Can Dream (Brown), 1968 — single, A-side (*Elvis TV Special* sessions)

21. If That Isn't Love (D. Rambo), 1973 — *Good Times*

SONG (COMPOSER), YEAR RECORDED ALBUM

22. If the Lord Wasn't Walking by My Side (Slaughter), 1966	*How Great Thou Art*
23. If We Never Meet Again (Brumley), 1960	*His Hand in Mine*
24. I Got a Feelin' in My Body (Linde), 1973	*Good Times*
25. I, John (Johnson, McFadden, Brooks), 1971	*He Touched Me*
26. I Just Can't Make It by Myself (Brewster), 1956	*The Million Dollar Quartet*
27. I'm Gonna Walk Them Golden Stairs (Holt), 1960	*His Hand in Mine*
28. In My Father's House (Hanks), 1960	*His Hand in Mine*
29. In the Garden (Miles), 1966	*How Great Thou Art*
30. In the Ghetto (Davis), 1969	*From Memphis to Vegas*
31. I Shall Not Be Moved (Benton), 1956	*The Million Dollar Quartet*
32. It Is No Secret (What God Can Do) (Hamblen), 1957	*Peace in the Valley*
33. I've God Confidence (Crouch), 1971	*He Touched Me*
34. Jesus Walked That Lonesome Valley (trad.), 1956	*The Million Dollar Quartet*
35. Joshua Fit the Battle (trad.), 1960	*His Hand in Mine*

SONG (COMPOSER), YEAR RECORDED ALBUM

36. Just a Little Talk with Jesus
(Derricks), 1956

The Million Dollar Quartet

37. Known Only to Him
(Hamblen), 1960

His Hand in Mine

38. Lead Me, Guide Me (Akers), 1971

He Touched Me

39. Let Us Pray (Weisman, Kaye), 1969

You'll Never Walk Alone

40. Mansion over the Hilltop
(Stanphill), 1960

His Hand in Mine

41. Milky White Way (trad.), 1960

His Hand in Mine

42. Miracle of the Rosary (Denson), 1971

Elvis Now

43. Nearer, My God, to Thee
(Fuller, Adams, Mason), 1972

Amazing Grace

44. Oh Happy Day (Doddridge, trad.),
1970

That's the Way It Is

45. Oh, How I Love Jesus (Whitfield),
1855

Platinum: A Life in Music

46. Only Believe (Rader), 1970

single, B-side

47. On the Jericho Road (trad.), 1956

The Million Dollar Quartet

48. Peace in the Valley (Dorsey), 1956

The Million Dollar Quartet

49. Put Your Hand in the Hand
(MacLellan), 1971

Elvis Now

SONG (COMPOSER), YEAR RECORDED ALBUM

50. Reach Out to Jesus (Carmichael), 1971 *He Touched Me*

51. Run On (trad.), 1966 *How Great Thou Art*

52. Seeing Is Believing (West, Spreen), 1971 *He Touched Me*

53. Show Me Thy Ways, O Lord (Shade), 1966 (home recording)

54. Sing, You Children (Nelson, Burch), 1967 *Easy Come, Easy Go*

55. Softly and Tenderly (Thompson), 1956 *The Million Dollar Quartet*

56. So High (trad.), 1966 *How Great Thou Art*

57. Somebody Bigger than You and I (Lange, Heath, Burke), 1966 *How Great Thou Art*

58. Stand by Me (trad.), 1966 *How Great Thou Art*

59. Swing Down, Sweet Chariot (trad.), 1960 *His Hand in Mine*

60. Take My Hand, Precious Lord (Dorsey), 1957 *Peace in the Valley* EP

61. The Lord's Prayer (Malotte, trad.), 1971 *A Hundred Years from Now*

62. There Is No God but God (Kenny), 1971 *He Touched Me*

63. Turn Your Eyes Upon Jesus (Lemmel, Clark), 1972 *Amazing Grace*

SONG (COMPOSER), YEAR RECORDED ALBUM

64. Up above My Head/Saved (medley; Lieber and Stoller), 1968	*Elvis TV Special* sessions
65. Walk a Mile in My Shoes (South), 1970	*On Stage*
66. We Call on Him (Karger, Weisman, Wayne), 1967	single, B-side
67. Where Could I Go but to the Lord (Coats), 1966	*How Great Thou Art*
68. Where No One Stands Alone (M. Lister, Tharp), 1966	*How Great Thou Art*
69. Why Me, Lord (Kristoffersen), 1974	*Live on Stage in Memphis*
70. Without Him (Lefevre), 1966	*How Great Thou Art*
71. Working on the Building (Hoyle, Bowles), 1960	*His Hand in Mine*
72. You Better Run (trad.), 1972	*Amazing Grace*
73. You Gave Me a Mountain (Robbins), 1973	*Aloha from Hawaii*
74. You'll Never Walk Alone (Rodgers and Hammerstein), 1967	single, B-side

Appendix B

Las Vegas Show script (see Introduction, pages 4–6). This is a script from the shows we did with Elvis after Las Vegas at the International Hotel, in 1970. The Colonel decided to do some personal appearances in the Northwest. For the fans who could not make it to Las Vegas, we took the Vegas show to them. Note the signature statement at the end: "Ladies and Gentlemen, Elvis has left the building."

1. The Statesmen Quartet circa mid-1950s. This photo shows Jake Hess and Jim "Big Chief" Wetherington. Jake was one of Elvis' favorite lead singers and song stylists. Big Chief is credited as the bass singer with hand and leg movements that had an early influence on Elvis. Jake would later go on to form The Imperials.

2. Blackwood Brothers Quartet circa 1954. This is the quartet that brought national attention to Southern-style male quartet singing. Their piano player, Jackie Marshall, set the bar by which all quartet pianists would be measured. Note the airplane in the background. Soon after this photo, this plane crashed and took the lives of R. W. Blackwood and Bill Lyles. This loss opened the door for J. D. Sumner to join the Blackwood Brothers as their new bass singer, and Cecil Blackwood to join as the new baritone. Cecil had been singing with the Songfellows, the group that auditioned Elvis.

3. The Harmoneers circa 1960. I joined this group from Atlanta, Georgia, my first foray into performing gospel. I was with this group the first time I met Elvis Presley. Elvis appeared at a show where we were performing and I approached him for an autograph, only to have Elvis ask that we trade. He wanted my autograph!

4. Joe Moscheo singing circa 1960. I am singing with the Harmoneers at an all-night singing in Atlanta, Georgia.

5. The Blackwood Brothers circa 1955. Here they appear with Cecil Blackwood and J. D. Sumner, who joined them after the plane crash took the lives of two members.

6. J. D. Sumner and the Stamps circa mid-1960s. Tony Brown and Donnie Sumner would later become members of Voice. Mylon LeFevre wrote "Without Him," which Elvis recorded on his *How Great Thou Art* album. Jimmy Blackwood is the son of James Blackwood, the original lead singer with the

Blackwood Brothers, who sang at the funeral of Elvis' mother, Gladys Presley.

7. The Original Jordanaires circa 1952. This is the group we all credit for bringing the style, rhythm, and feel of black spirituals to a white audience. Elvis was very familiar with their arrangements and often referred to them. The Matthews brothers were a big part of the sound. Gordon Stoker played piano for the group and sang tenor. Gordon went on to organize the group Elvis would invite to join him as his backup singers for the next fifteen years.

8. The Blackwood Brothers with Elvis Presley circa 1955. This is an early photo of James Blackwood, Jackie Marshall, J. D. Sumner, and R. W. Blackwood with Elvis at the National Quartet Convention in Memphis.

9. Record jacket of The Imperials with Jake Hess. This recording was released as a single. The song was written by Jerry Reed on the Impact label, an imprint of Heart Warming Records that was created for us.

10. The Jordanaires backing Elvis Presley in the studio. The Jordanaires backed Elvis in the studio when he recorded for fifteen years.

11. *His Hand in Mine* album cover. This was the first full-length gospel album Elvis recorded in 1960.

12. If I Can Dream. In this photo Elvis is performing the powerfully moving song "If I Can Dream," which was recorded before a live audience at the NBC Studio for the *Elvis* television special in 1968—the first time Elvis had performed live in ten years. This is my all-time favorite song Elvis sang. His performance has been so inspiring to me.

13. "How Great Thou Art" sheet music. "How Great Thou Art" had been recorded by many artists and was always featured on the Billy Graham Crusades. When Elvis recorded it he took it to a new level.

14. *How Great Thou Art* album cover. Elvis received the first Grammy of his career for this recording. The Imperials and the Jordainaires served as backing vocalists on this album.

15. Grammy for *How Great Thou Art*. Elvis' first of three Grammys, all of which were for his gospel recordings.

16. International Hotel sign. This is for the show opening in August of 1969. Elvis was always kind to share his "space" with his singers and musicians.

17. The Imperials. This configuration of The Imperials opened for Elvis Presley in 1969 at the International Hotel in Las Vegas. (Armond Morales, Jim Murray, Elvis, me, Terry Blackwood, and Roger Wiles in front.)

18. After-show gathering in Elvis' suite. Elvis invited us up to his suite even though we were performing with Jimmy Dean at the time. Mama Cass asked us to back her on "Amazing Grace."

19. Sweet Inspirations with Cissy Houston. This configuration of the Sweet Inspirations opened for Elvis Presley in 1969 at the International Hotel in Las Vegas.

20. Dove Award. This is the award The Imperials received for Best Male Group in 1969. After we received this award Elvis had a new way of introducing us for every show.

21. Imperials with Dove Award. "A proud group." Winning this award was confirmation for us that our music was being heard, and was important.

22. Joe accepting Dove Award. In 1969 The Imperials were given the Dove Award for Best Male Gospel Group. From that point on Elvis Presley would introduce us in this way: "Ladies and Gentlemen, the Best Male Gospel Group in America, The Imperials."

23. Elvis in rehearsal with cast for 1969 opening at the International Hotel. This was a week before going into the main show room to rehearse with the full orchestra.

24. Elvis with The Imperials prior to a show at the International Hotel. This photo was taken in front of The Imperials' dressing room.

25. Elvis with The Imperials prior to a show.

26. Elvis with The Imperials backstage at the Landmark Hotel in Las Vegas. This is the hotel where we were performing with Jimmy Dean. He is wearing his "attendance record belt," which was awarded to him by the City of Las Vegas. Larry Gatlin, who was singing with us at the time, is at the far right.

27. *He Touched Me* album cover. This album won a Grammy and included six songs previously recorded by The Imperials. The Imperials backed Elvis on this great album of gospel songs. Bill Gaither wrote the title song, "He Touched Me."

28. Elvis Presley and Joe Moscheo circa 1969. Elvis and me at a happy moment backstage in Las Vegas.

29. Joe Moscheo with J. D. Sumner circa 1968. Before either Joe or J.D. had gone to work for Elvis, J.D. had a booking agency in Nashville called Sumar that booked dates for several gospel groups, including The Imperials. I worked for J.D. as a talent scout for the agency. Neither of us had any idea of the connection we would each have with Elvis in the future.

30. The Imperials, including Sherman Andrus. Sherman joined the group in 1972.

31. The Imperials. In this photo, we are waiting to go on for a network TV appearance.

32. Personal note from Elvis to Joe after family tragedy. Elvis was always very generous and kind to those around him. He was particularly supportive when we were facing personal struggles and always wanted to do what he could to help us through them.

33. The Imperials. This is a promotional photo of The Imperials at the height of our popularity in Contemporary Christian Music. Note from the top of the photo that we were with the Sumar Talent Agency.

34. The Stamps. This photo depicts the Stamps as they first appeared with Elvis Presley in Las Vegas. Richard Sterban would go on to sing bass with the Oak Ridge Boys.

35. Elvis show ad. This ad ran in a magazine to promote Elvis' show. Note his generosity in promoting us before him.

36. The Stamps with Elvis. This photo was taken at the International Hotel in Las Vegas.

37. Elvis Las Vegas newspaper ad. Since the shows were always a sell-out, Elvis and the Colonel would place ads in all the local newspapers to say "thank you." It was always surprising to see our names bigger than Elvis'—another example of his generosity.

38. Joe Moscheo and Priscilla Presley. Priscilla accompanied me to the 1976 Grammy Awards in Los Angeles. She is always popular with the paparazzi.

39. Copy of speech Joe gave at Elvis' induction into the Gospel Music Hall of Fame. The estate was kind enough to allow me, Gordon Stoker, and Ed Enoch to present the Hall of Fame honor to Jack Soden, who represented the Elvis Presley Estate when this award was given.

40. Souvenir menu cover and interior #1. A different menu was created for each of Elvis Presley's appearances in the show room. These "souvenir" menus have become collectors' items.

41. Souvenir menu cover and interior #2.

42. Backstage passes for cast members and crew. The rectangular pass is one from the 1969 tour, right after the show in Las Vegas. The appearance of these passes changed significantly throughout the years. The early passes were for all involved, but later passes distinguished between the show cast and crew members.

43. The Imperials certificate of induction into GMA Gospel Music Hall of Fame.

44. Award given to The Imperials at induction into GMA Gospel Music Hall of Fame.

45. Award presented to Joe Moscheo for production of the DVD *He Touched Me: The Gospel Music of Elvis*.

46. Award presented to Joe Moscheo for Gold video status of *He Touched Me* DVD. Presented to Joe Moscheo to commemorate RIAA certified gold sales of more than 50,000 units of the long-form video, February 2001.

47. The Imperials today. This is our most recent publicity photo. We are still traveling and performing around the world. Gus Gaches is singing tenor with us. Terry Blackwood, Sherman Andrus, and I have been together for thirty-five years.

48. "All Access" memorabilia.

INDEX

ABOUT THE AUTHOR

Joe Moscheo joined The Imperials in 1964, a gospel quartet that participated in Elvis' Las Vegas show as one of his backup groups and also on many of his recordings. He spent four years with Elvis as a performer, but became a friend for life. Joe later held the position of vice-president of Special Projects with BMI, ran his own artist-management agency, is currently president of MCS America, Inc., and still travels with some of The Imperials doing EP fan-club events around the world. With the full support of Elvis Presley Enterprises, he co-produced the DVD *He Touched Me: The Gospel Music of Elvis* in 2001 and the recently released *Elvis Lives: The 25th Anniversary Concert* DVD. Joe lives in Nashville, Tennessee, with his family. For more information you can visit these Web sites: www.joemoscheo.net, www.theimperials.us, www.elvis.com.